Betty,
This book is
dedicated to you,
a fellow warrior
Always look for
His joy on your
journey!

GET IN THE BOAT!
Finding hope and humor in the midst of the storm.

2 Cor. 4: 8-10 & 16-18

Judy Gerdis

Chairein!

Judy Gerdis

XUl

TABLE OF CONTENTS

❈

Part I GETTING IN THE BOAT

DEDICATION

To all warriors who have fought and will fight the tireless battle to maintain hope and a sense of humor when asked to go through the storm. May your boat be kept afloat by the almighty hand of God and may you never waver in your perseverance to get to the other side, whether it be in this life or the next.

ACKNOWLEDGMENTS

I could have never faced my storm without the support and prayers offered up on my behalf by all my friends and family. Thanks to my wonderful Empower Bible Class at Southeast Christian Church in Louisville, Kentucky for their unwavering care and concern, the delicious meals and transportation to and from treatments. To my SECC "pew-mates" and Reta Stivers and Linda Igleheart for their ability to make me laugh in the midst of the agony. To my friend and pen-pal, Kevin Taylor, who continually supported me in prayer and consistently sent cards and letters to bolster my faith. To old friends from my childhood at Hillcrest Children's Home in Hot Springs, and my Covenant family.

To the First Baptist Church of Royal for covering me with love and prayers when they didn't even know me. To the congregation of Mount Hermon United Methodist Church who knitted and crocheted the lovely prayer shawls. To the believers of the Maasai tribe in Kenya and particularly the chief who continues to pray for my protection along with the students and staff of The Rift Valley Academy. To Joel and Toby for their suggestion that I change the title and launch out into the deep end of trust. To my husband for all the nights he stayed up to pray that I could make it another day. And finally, special thanks is given to my closest buddies, Yvonne Perry Clark for her untiring love, and Donna Gunnoe for never missing a single treatment day and helping me edit and prepare this book for publishing. I will never be able to thank you enough.

ENDORSEMENTS

I have known Judy Gerdis for many years and prayed for her regularly during her ordeal with cancer. However, I didn't know what to expect when she asked me to read her book about her experience.

As a guy, I didn't expect to be absorbed by a book about women with breast cancer, the demoralizing effects of losing their hair, or the side effects of chemotherapy. However, not only is this a good story of faith and courage, but it provides practical, Biblical insights for cancer victims and those who support and encourage them. I'd say it is a must read for men and women who have a family member or close personal friend with a diagnosis, or for anyone who wants to better understand this debilitating disease.

Don Waddell

New Member Minister and The Outlook columnist

Southeast Christian Church

Louisville, Kentucky

Praises to Judy for opening our eyes to the horrible disease of breast cancer. She has shared her heart, dreams, anxieties, fears, emotions and yet gives God glory through all the ups and downs of this difficult time in her life. Laced with scripture, and through tears and laughter, she shares with the reader insights about this dreaded and disfiguring disease. An excellent read for friends and family who have loved ones facing traumatic times.

Judy Russell

Bob Russell Ministries

I just finished reading Judy's very open and courageous story about her battle with breast cancer. Through her gifted writing, she forces you to walk through it with her on every level; the horror and the humor of it all; the expected and the totally unexpected!

You will laugh and cry with her as she makes herself vulnerable to her reading audience, as she shares the lows and the highs on every level; emotionally, mentally, physically, spiritually, and financially. I am a better person because Judy allowed me, as a reader, to experience this with her, her family, her faithful old friends, as well as the new ones she met along her journey. As a result I have found a new level of compassion for what the "pink" is all about! Breast cancer is not for sissies! Thank you Judy for your honesty about your painful experiences and for the side-splitting humor! I wholeheartedly recommend this book to male and female alike.

Carol Agee

Author of "The Kingdom of God Where is the Fruit?"

Woman of Excellence Teacher

Life Skills teacher in Kentucky Prisons

PART I

GETTING IN THE BOAT

GOD'S PROMISE

✷

T oward the end of August 2008, on one of my days off from selling patio homes for a builder, I ambled into my favorite store at one of the malls in Louisville, Kentucky. I had been trying to be good in light of the recent economic downturn and had stayed away from the shopping scene for several weeks, but a $30 coupon had enticed me to drive the 20 miles into town from my home in Shelbyville, Kentucky.

I intended to stay for only a few minutes, but it seemed others had the same idea. The store was crowded with women going through neatly stacked garments on tables and rainbow-hued racks of clothing. I found a couple of outfits, and after trying them on, I made my way to the cash register.

As I waited my turn, one of the clerks showed me a pink box that contained two beautiful pale-pink, beaded bracelets. They were part of a campaign to raise funds to fight breast cancer. On each bracelet dangled a silver charm with the word *promise* engraved in black letters. I immediately thought of little Maia, our unborn granddaughter in New Jersey, because we had just learned she would be born in November with hypo plastic right heart syndrome (HRHS).

Hypo plastic right heart syndrome is a congenital heart defect in which the right ventricle of the heart fails to grow and develop appropriately. The underdeveloped ventricle cannot contain the proper amount of blood pumped from the right atrium. The ventricle's muscle structure is poor, which creates additional problems as the heart attempts to pump blood to the pulmonary valve for transfer to the lungs. From the reports, it looked like she also had a hole in her heart. We knew at birth Mia would need immediate emergency treatment, because her heart would probably begin to fail with her first breath.

I bought a box of two bracelets, one to keep for myself and the other to send to my daughter, Trina. I knew the bracelet would be a good reminder to pray for this precious child and connect me to Trina over the difficult months ahead.

Maia Elisabeth was to be my granddaughter's full name. When I returned home, I looked up the meaning of both names and found that *Maia* means "mine," and *Elisabeth* means "God's oath" or "God's promise." What a coincidence! I nearly jumped out of my seat with excitement. God seemed to be saying that Maia was His promise.

The next day, I returned to the store and purchased 10 boxes, 20 bracelets, and gave them to friends so they could use the tiny pink beads as a reminder to help me pray for our granddaughter. I had no idea those bracelets would be worn as a reminder to pray for me too, and that some of them would not come off the wrists of my friends for nearly a year. I didn't have a clue that my journey, along with Maia's, had just begun.

STATISTICS DON'T
APPLY ANYMORE

In 1996, I had a mammogram indicating a calcium malformation in my left breast. My general doctor couldn't feel any abnormalities, but he decided to refer me to a surgeon — just to be safe. The surgeon couldn't detect any lumps, but he chose to do a biopsy anyway. As I was released from the hospital, the surgeon told me his nurse would call in three days to let me know the results.

I will never forget the moment the phone rang. I was in the bathroom preparing for work, and Tom, my husband of 29 years, answered. When I heard him say, "Yes, Dr. Hoagland, I'll get her," I knew something wasn't right. Why would the doctor call rather than have the nurse do it? I picked up the phone, and as I looked at my reflection in the mirror, I heard these words: "Well, I have good news, and I have bad news. The bad news is it turned out to be cancer after all. The good news is that it's confined to the ducts, and there are a myriad options for you to consider."

Immediately, I remembered that during a private devotional two months earlier I had felt a still small voice say, "You are going to go through something soon that might frighten you. Don't be afraid because I am going to be with you, and you will come through it victorious."

Oh, then I'm going to be all right. I thought to myself as I continued putting on my face. Tom was still on the phone, and I heard him ask, "What are the options, Doctor?"

"Anything from a radical mastectomy to doing nothing," was the reply.

Who can explain what goes through a person's mind at a time like that? I recall thinking, *since there isn't any history of cancer in my family, I'll do nothing.*

I realize now that to think so stupidly was very irrational on my part, but I was busy, both with my work and with family matters. My husband's mother had become critically ill in Connecticut, and my father had just suffered a stroke and was in a hospital in Cape Girardeau, Missouri. I had too many other irons in the fire to worry about a cancer confined to the ducts. Besides, we were scheduled to leave within a week to fly to England and Wales. No, I decided, I'll do nothing.

Tom wasn't too sure that was my best option, so he scheduled a conference with the surgeon. We discussed every possibility and every option. I kept trying to get the doctor to tell me what he would do if his wife were in the same situation, but he hesitated to answer. Finally, after 20 minutes of coaxing, he said, "If you were my wife, I'd have you do a lumpectomy followed up with six weeks of radiation therapy."

All right then, I had an answer! He encouraged us to go ahead with our travel plans, pray about our decision, and tell him what we wanted to do when we returned.

I made a quick weekend trip to Missouri to be with my parents before we were to leave the country. Many decisions had to be made concerning my father's care, and my mother needed me in person to give her support. I sat next to Mom in my father's semiprivate room at St. Francis Hospital in Cape Girardeau. My mother knew about my biopsy, so as soon as we had a spare moment to ourselves she asked about the result. I told her it was cancer, but it wasn't a big deal, emphasizing it was confined to the ducts. Then I made the comment that since no one in our family had ever had cancer, I probably wouldn't have anything done.

My head was turned away from my mother when I heard her say, "You know, Judy, you might want to reconsider your decision because your grandmother Bruhn died of breast cancer."

My head nearly whipped off my neck. What was she saying? I blurted, "You never told me that!"

"Oh, yes!" she continued. "Before we went to Alaska in 1945 your grandmother Bruhn showed me her nipples. They were inverted and oozing fluid. Your grandfather wouldn't allow her to go to the doctor. I've always thought she died of breast cancer, but because she never saw a doctor I wasn't sure."

I was reeling with emotion. Stunned would be more like it. All kinds of thoughts raced through my head. This put a new twist on the decision I had to make.

We headed for England a few days later. Ironically, we were scheduled to stay with two surgeons and their families we had met while they were studying at the University of Louisville. The first was Dr. Tim Brown in Swansea, Wales. While we were with him and his wife, Sue, I shared my dilemma. Easter Sunday, Tim called one of his friends who was the foremost cancer surgeon in Wales. His suggestion, after hearing the findings, was the same as Dr. Hoagland's.

Later in the week, we were with Dr. Mike and Sarah Waldrum in Birmingham, England. Even though Mike is a hand surgeon, it was good to hear his opinion of my situation. He agreed with the conclusions of the other two surgeons. That was it. On the plane back to the States, I prayed and felt the Lord telling me to follow Dr. Hoagland's plan. Everything was going to be okay. I had no qualms. I was at peace.

Prior to having surgery, I had an appointment with my general physician, Dr. Nanine Henderson. She appeared very concerned at the diagnosis, so for some reason I tried to lighten the mood by telling her my initial response not to do anything. She recoiled with horror, "Judy, statistics don't apply to you anymore. It doesn't matter that no one in your family has had cancer. You have cancer now!"

I sat up straight and felt like I had been slapped in the face. The old commercial, "Thanks. I needed that!" played in my head, She was right of course. It didn't matter anymore. I had cancer.

I went through that season of my life in a bubble of confidence. I never missed a day of work because I scheduled the surgeries on my days off. I had the radiation treatments every morning before work five days a week for six weeks. It was so easy and so uneventful I actually didn't consider myself to be a breast-cancer survivor. It was just another bump (or *lump* in this case) in the road. I didn't think I was worthy to be counted among those who really had fought the fight. Women like my good friend Mary.

MARY, MARY

I met Mary through a Bible class at our church. A year later, she was diagnosed with a rare form of breast cancer, Padget's disease and inflammatory breast cancer, which begin as a rash. When she was diagnosed with this insidious cancer, Mary was given 10 months to live.

Mary dearly wanted to see her twin daughters, Ashley and Brittany, graduate from high school in 2009. Her race to the goal began with her applying to any medical trial that would accept her and seeking approval to take the latest and strongest drugs on the market (and those not yet on the market in some cases). Never wavering in her attempt to live just a little longer, Mary became a human test tube.

During her struggle to survive, Mary displayed a beautiful Christ-like spirit of joy and humility. She consoled her family and friends when the prognosis looked most dire. Mary expressed unfailing faith in the One who made her and held her in the palm of His hand. The joy of her relationship with her God flooded her face and was a constant source of awe for those who watched her struggle.

A month following her initial diagnosis, Mary's husband, Doug, fell on his head at a construction site. That accident resulted in numerous operations and ended with his experiencing double vision and seizures that left him unable to drive. Mary wouldn't hear of any of us driving Doug to his appointments; she insisted on taking care of his every need herself.

While dealing with Mary's treatments and Doug's disability, one of the twins, Brittany, developed seizures that occurred as often as five times a minute. The family traveled to St. Louis for treatment for her and stumbled onto a medication that held the tremors and seizures at bay.

Mary's cancer went into remission three times. Three times she praised the Lord for a clean scan and positive doctors' reports. Unfortunately, the last time the cancer returned, it was with a vengeance. As I prayed for Mary through the years, I only imagined the cruel lesions under the veil of Mary's blouse. One night after Bible class, Mary took me out into the hall and ever so gently pulled apart the buttons and bared the ugly truth for me to see with my own eyes. At that moment, I knew I would never be the same. Looking at the open tumors and experiencing the odor of rotting flesh, I changed. I changed the way I prayed, and I changed the way I cared.

Mary was told in June 2008 a new medical trial might accept her into their experimental program. We were asked to pray that she would be allowed to participate in one more attempt to find a cure. She was accepted, but the trial wasn't scheduled to begin until August, and she was tired and weary of the fight. Mary faced her mortality head on, indicating a desire to go Home and enter into His perfect peace. She remained in the hospital for her final days, and Doug called his daughters home from the summer Kentucky Governor's Scholars Program. Even through the final days, Mary was able to share with numerous people her personal relationship with God through Jesus.

As soon as the twins returned to town, their school, Christian Academy of Louisville, set in motion a plan to have a "pregraduation" ceremony in the hospital's chapel so Mary could realize her dream of seeing her daughters graduate. Within a 24-hour period, preparations were made, and Mary was wheeled down the corridor into the chapel, which was crowded with friends and family. She was stunned and amazed that so much had been planned in such a short time. Newspapers, TV, and radio stations were all on hand to witness and report on the moving ceremony. The girls marched to "Pomp and Circumstance," wearing their graduation gowns, caps, and tassels. Mary beamed. Cameramen wept. Not a dry eye could be found in the chapel.

The national press picked up the story, and Mary's "dream come true" was seen all over the Midwest. After the ceremony ended, Mary sat patiently answering questions and sharing her strong faith in the Lord. Then she was wheeled to her room where she rested, and her rapid decline began. Only a few days later Mary breathed her last and flew into the arms of Jesus.

Hundreds of people came to Mary's visitations. The family received cards and letters from all over the United States. The funeral was a glorious celebration of her life and a testament to her faith. At the conclusion, an invitation was given to those who did not know Mary's Lord to accept Him as their Savior.

Tom and I used to sing a song titled "May Christ Be Seen in Me," and I believe the words perfectly epitomize Mary's mission in life:

Oh, Lord, I give myself to thee

And all that I possess.

I lay aside my sinful self

And claim thy righteousness.

My will lies shattered at thy feet.

I pray thy will be done.

My only plea, to live for thee

And magnify thy Son.

Oh, humbly may I serve thee Lord

As in thy will I tread.

And may I live anew in Christ

As risen from the dead.

Then closely walking by thy side

May love flow out through me.

That those whom thou shall send my way

May too find life in thee.

May Christ be seen in me, Oh Lord.

Hear thou my earnest plea.

Oh, take me. Use me. Fill me Lord.

Til Christ be seen in me.[1]

What an impact Mary had on my life. I wondered if I had to walk a similar path, would I be able to carry myself with such grace and dignity? I wondered what I would do if I faced the same challenges.

GOING THROUGH
✸

In 2006, I had a routine mammogram. The results showed extensive calcium deposits. Normally, the news would not have bothered me, but because 13 years earlier I had been diagnosed with Stage I ductile cancer in my left breast, my first reaction was to ask for a biopsy. Doctors explained because the calcifications were so numerous and dense, doing a biopsy would be utterly impossible, requiring numerous needle punctures that would turn my breast into a sieve. If I insisted, they would try to modify the procedure, putting me on my stomach with my breast forced through a hole in a table. The consensus was that it would be much more advantageous if I just had a mammogram every six months, allowing doctors to compare films to determine if there had been any changes. Consequently, every six months, I drove to the diagnostic-imaging facility in DuPont Circle and endured the squeezing, compressing, and squishing of my breasts as the "vice" turned my glands into pancakes. Having fibromyalgia complicated the process, and on two occasions I nearly passed out from pain.

A few days after my fateful trip to the mall and purchasing the "promise" bracelets, I was due to have my regular six-month mammogram. I remember sitting outside the office building in my car, trying to dredge up the courage to go inside. Before I could take the elevator up to the second floor, my cell phone rang. A voice on the other end said, "What are you up to?"

"I'm trying to gather my courage to face the mammogram monster. That's what," I moaned. When I explained how painful it was for me, my friend prayed I wouldn't have any pain at all this time. I thought, *Oh, right. Like that is going to do any good.* I was actually quite surprised I had very little discomfort when the nurse technician clamped the machine down for the mammography.

"You are good!" I smiled with surprise.

"Yup. They tell me I'm the best," she beamed.

Two days later I received a call saying they needed me to return for a magnification. I'd had similar calls before, so I wasn't concerned. The appointment was scheduled for the following day. The "promise" charm dangled from my wrist as I stood with my breast squished flat. I gazed at the wall beside the imaging machine where the nurse had clipped the previous film. My head was cocked to the side, so I could get a better look as I examined what appeared to be a mass of white, gray, and black dots. I would never pretend to know the first thing about reading X-rays, but what I saw stunned me. I thought, *my goodness! I can even see something is there. What is that?*

The nurse finished with the pictures. I pulled the gown up over my shoulders, and I turned to leave. She said, "Oh, Mrs. Gerdis, you aren't finished. We need you to have an ultrasound before you go." She escorted me down the hall and through two sets of doors to a small windowless room where she instructed me to lie on an examination table. She rubbed the gel over my right breast and proceeded to move the wand slowly over my skin, stopping every so often to click a picture. Each time she pushed into my skin, I winced with pain.

I told myself, "That's a good sign. Right? Pain? Cancer isn't supposed to be painful to the touch. Yes," I convinced myself. "It's a good sign."

The technician finished, and I sat on the side of the table while she took the slides and previewed them via a screen on the wall. I watched and took note as best I could. Umm . . . . Where had I seen similar images? Oh, yes, it was on Oprah.

Dr. Oz had shown slides of cancer cells. Well, I'm just imagining things. "Judy, get a grip."

"How long before I'll know the results of the ultrasound?" I questioned, staring at the slides before me.

"Oh, I'm going to get the doctor right now, so you'll know in a few minutes." The tech exited the room.

I stared at my feet. I stood up and rearranged my gown. Then I hummed a little tune and decided if I acted like nothing was going to come of this, perhaps I could just will it away. After all, I had no business interpreting mammogram film, and I certainly didn't know a thing about ultrasound pictures. I thought of Trina who was probably going through an ultrasound in Philadelphia about the same time. Was she getting a close look at Maia? Could they see her little ventricles and valves?

The doctor swept into the room and got right down to business. "The film I've seen today indicates a need for further examination. My recommendation is that you have a biopsy."

"How soon?"

"Soon."

"Will I need to be hospitalized for this?"

"We can do it right here in the office, if you like."

Remembering my previous experience, I mentioned I'd like to have Dr. Hoagland do the biopsy. We agreed I would contact Dr. Hoagland and let their office know the plans.

I got dressed and went out to pay my portion of the bill. Was it my imagination or did the other techs and nurses avert their eyes and lower their voices when I stood at the desk? I'm sure it was my imagination. As soon as I got home I looked up Dr. Hoagland's number and called his office. I explained what had just transpired and asked if the receptionist could relay the message and have the doctor return my call as soon as possible. The doctor called within the hour and said he would be happy to do the procedure, but his schedule was crammed with surgeries and appointments for the next two weeks. To avoid delay, he thought it would be good for me to have the biopsy done at the diagnostic office, saying he fully trusted the other doctor's ability to take care of me. I called and set up the appointment for the first part of the following week.

By that time, we had heard from Trina concerning her appointment in Philadelphia for her ultrasound and consultation with the surgeons who would be delivering Maia and caring for her. They had scheduled a C-section for the end of October. Tom and I discussed traveling to be with the family to help care for our four-year-old grandson, Gideon. The protocol immediately after Maia's birth would allow Trina and her husband, Kenny, to hold her a few minutes before she was whisked away to the NICU for tests. They would watch her for two to three days and then decide whether to do a valvoplasty or shunt. There was concern the tricuspid valve needed to grow. If it grew, she probably would not have to have the more invasive shunt operation.

The day of my biopsy, the pink-beaded bracelets were being worn by women (and one very brave man) all over the world. I had to leave mine in the changing room, but I took one last look at the "promise" charm. Then I padded my way back to the ultrasound room where I would endure the needle without the benefit of anesthesia. Even though the area was deadened, the procedure was not pleasant. I felt every tug and twist as they withdrew tissue samples from several areas of my right breast. Later, as I staggered out the door, the staff promised to call with the results in two days.

Two days after the biopsy, I sat reading a book in our family room and glanced at the clock every five minutes. When would they call? The ring caught me by surprise, and startled, I jumped from my seat to grasp the phone. Carrying the cordless receiver with me, I glanced out the back window and heard the radiologist say, "Mrs. Gerdis? It is cancer, but it is a medium grade and should be simple to treat. I'm sure you are going to be okay. But you do need to call your surgeon as soon as possible." I thanked her and pushed the "end" button to cancel the call. Standing there, looking at the multihued trees with leaves cascading onto our lawn, I felt calmer than I had 10 minutes earlier. After calling Tom, I dialed the surgeon. The receptionist was able to squeeze me in for an appointment the following Tuesday.

I chose Dr. Hoagland again because he and his wife pray for his patients every evening, and he prays with his patients before surgery. I had total confidence in his ability, and I felt he would understand how desperately I wanted to be available to our daughter and her family at Maia's birth. Trina and Kenny were going to need all the support we could give them as they faced unknown medical needs for a newborn and stamina to care for an active four year old. Because they lived and worked an hour's drive from The Children's Hospital of Philadelphia (CHOP), where Maia would be born, their lives were going to get complicated.

I questioned, but only for a moment, why I had to go through this crisis when other members of our family were about to experience hardships of a different nature. I was more than a little perplexed, but I had to believe God had a plan in all I was about to face. I sat down at the computer to check e-mails and send out a message requesting prayer. Before I could compose anything, I opened up a message that pertained to "going through". It said that anytime we go through something that seems hard to bear or even impossible to solve, we should think about the worst thing that had happened in our life and realize that with God's help we did make it through – we really did survive. I was told in the message to start rejoicing that with God's help I would overcome because this too would pass.

The day of my appointment, Tom and I met with Dr. Hoagland for about an hour and a half. It appeared from the ultrasound tests the tumor measured 16 millimeters. When I was told the size I had no frame of reference because the one aspect of my high school and college math classes that did not stick was the metric system. So the doctor methodically interpreted the findings, indicating the tumor was about half an inch in diameter. The cancer had invaded the exterior walls of the duct and now rested within the breast tissue.

The doctor's plan was to do a lumpectomy the following Thursday. I would arrive at 8:00 AM. At 10:00 AM, I would have a guide wire inserted. At the mention of the wire, I cringed. Dr. Hoagland saw I was immediately uncomfortable, and I reminded him that the last time they inserted the wire they missed the prime location and had to remove and reinsert the needle. He explained that the doctor who did the biopsy had implanted a chip that would help technicians pinpoint the exact spot, which should make this insertion go much smoother than the prior procedure. At 10:30 AM I would have a radioactive dye shot into the area so by the time the surgery began at 11:30 AM, the medical staff would know if any lymph nodes were contaminated.

The sentinel lymph-node biopsy is relatively new. In the old days, surgeons had to retrieve lymph nodes so they could be tested later. With the sentinel lymph-node biopsy, nodes are not removed unless the sentinel nodes are affected. Dr. Hoagland continued to explain if the nodes were compromised I would have to start chemotherapy immediately. If they were not, I would have a seven-week window before I had to start radiation therapy. The latter would allow us to make the trip to New Jersey to provide emotional support to Trina and Kenny and help care for Gideon. Just knowing the plan of action improved my peace level tremendously.

When I got home from the appointment, I had a message from a friend who had recently experienced the same journey. She said *Proverbs 5:21* had become her faith Scripture: "Look heavenward and realize that this arrangement is sovereignly put together for your good and for His glory"

(her version and interpretation). That sounded good to me.
Then I was reminded of a book excerpt I had read many
years earlier about a lady who had asked people to pray for
her husband who was undergoing an extremely dangerous
operation that he might not survive. When he survived and
recovered with full health, the lady's friends said to her, "Oh,
wasn't it good God spared your husband's life?" She thought
about this for a long time and finally came to the conclusion
God wasn't good to spare her husband's life. God was good .
. . PERIOD! God was good. He *is* good all the time. Not just
when things go our way. He is good. No matter the outcome
of the days and months ahead I had to remember, God *is*
good. He had me get in the boat for a purpose.

LAUGHING ALL THE WAY TO THE OR

❈

I walked back to the preop room at 8:45 AM. My family was not allowed to be with me until all the testing was complete. The guide-wire was inserted at 10:00, then I was taken further into the bowels of the hospital. (I say that because the hospital has become a huge medical facility with corridors off corridors, beneath passageways, over walkways, behind dungeons . . . 'just a massive complex.) The insertion of the radioactive dye was NOT the pleasant experience I was led to believe it would be, but it did happen right on schedule. By the time I got back to the preop room, two hours or more had elapsed, and Tom, Joel (my son), and Toby (my daughter-in-law) were wondering if they had somehow been forgotten as "the next of kin."

I was certainly glad to see them when they finally came into my small cubicle. We settled into the normal chitchat. Ron Yankee, a friend in the real-estate world, was working that day as part of our church's Care Ministry. He dropped by to talk and pray with us. Then Dr. Hoagland came by to see how we were doing. He let us know the OR was running just a little behind, but he was on his way to scrub up. He also took time to pray with me. My nurse had finished all her duties and only poked her head into the room to check on us every few minutes. The clock ticked off the seconds. It was about time to go.

Joel was standing near my gurney when I saw him look down at the floor by my bed. He nonchalantly took his foot and flipped something that went sailing across the room and landed under a chair. I stared. He stared. He started laughing and asked. "Is that what I think it is?" I told him it sure looked like it. He moved to the chair and bent down to get a closer look, and he laughed again. "Mom, that is a ball of poop!"

"No way!"

"Yes, way!"

We all started laughing uncontrollably. This could only happen to our family.

The subject of gas and poop has held a long-standing place in our conversations since Tom and I had our first date. He mistook a sewage-filled creek for "a moment of indiscretion" on my part. How dare he! As our three kids grew, and their "toots" slipped out, their common disclaimer was, "It's not me. It's the creek!" When the kids started dating, they would warn their prospective dates to expect family conversations to revert to personal hygiene within, oh, let's say, 15 minutes. Invariably their predictions proved to be right on the money. "Amazing!" would be the boyfriend's or girlfriend's reaction.

So just before my going to surgery, we laughed! We couldn't stop. Finally, I told Joel to get a paper towel and pick up the offensive solid and toss it in the trash can. He wasn't willing to do that. He claimed the nurse needed to know somehow, someway, this turd had found its way into the preop room. MY preop room! Joel pulled back the curtain and motioned to one of the nurses that we needed someone to come to our room. One of them responded to our bidding and arrived at the exact same moment as the orderly who had been assigned to push me to the operating room. Both looked inside the room, and Joel pointed to the brown ball still under the chair. The nurse looked quite shocked, and before she could stop herself she blurted out a profanity. We laughed even more. She apologized, and I said, "You know, normally I detest that word, but in this situation it is quite appropriate!" We laughed even harder.

It was true! Having been raised in a preacher's home, I was never allowed to even say "by-words," and I had impressed on my children that out of the mouth the abundance of the heart speaks (*Matt. 12:34*, paraphrase). For me, some words were abhorrent, and that was one of them.

The nurse said, "I was wondering why y'all were laughing. We aren't accustomed to having people laugh while they are waiting to have surgery." By that time the young orderly was standing outside the door holding his sides as his body shook out of control. He actually was sliding down the wall to a crouched position because his legs wouldn't support his weight. Of course, the biggest question was, how did this get here? No one knew. It was a mystery. Joel knew it couldn't have been there the whole time because someone would have noticed it and/or stepped on it. (In it?) The orderly tried to stand, but he was still bent over with tears streaming down his cheeks; however, he couldn't linger, I had to go to the operating room. As my family stifled their mirth, they each gave me a kiss goodbye. Just as I was whisked away to surgery, the nurse grabbed some elastic gloves, picked up the turd, and threw it in the trash.

I chuckled all the way down the hall and into the OR. Everyone looked stunned as both the orderly and I entered the room shaking, not from nerves or the cold, but from laughter. The orderly explained what had happened, making sure to add grand embellishments and a nervous twitter took over the room. As the mask went over my face, I heard someone accuse Dr. Hoagland of the mysterious deed. I gasped for air to let out a,"Ha," and that was the last I remembered.

SEND IN THE CLOWNS

I spent the night at the hospital. The radioactive dye injected for the test had lit up the sentinel nodes, so Dr. Hoagland took those and five lymph nodes. He also widened the lumpectomy to gather tissue outside the perimeters. He said he would let me know the results of the test by the first of the following week. Before being discharged from the hospital the doctor who would be my oncologist visited my room. He methodically went over the type of treatment I would receive depending on the results of the tissue/node tests. Since the sentinel nodes were involved, it meant my treatment would definitely include chemo, followed up with radiation. The exact number of chemo sessions and the days or weeks separating those treatments would not be known until the pathology reports were reviewed. I went home with a drainage tube and a fluid-collection bulb that would be removed after a week. Tom and I had to empty the fluid and measure it carefully. When a day's fluid totaled less than 30 ccs, I could go back to the surgeon's office and have the tube removed.

We received a call from Trina telling us the doctors had decided Maia would be born October 29. She and Kenny had met with the cardiac team, toured the cardiac care unit (CCU), and visited the Ronald McDonald House where they would be staying. They learned a shuttle bus would take them back and forth between the Ronald McDonald House and CHOP.

Their morning had started with an echo cardiogram of Maia's heart, and according to what the doctors saw, the tricuspid valve had widened a little bit. That little change signaled that Maia would probably need fewer surgeries than previously expected. They also did an amniocentesis to see if there might be a genetic predisposition to hypo plastic right heart syndrome. In addition, they met with one of the nurses and a social worker representing a philanthropic group whose mission is to assist couples facing tremendously high and outstanding medical bills.

I was relieved to know the Lord was working in Maia's little heart, and knowing that made the wait to hear about my lab reports less of an anxious ordeal. However, I never got a call from the doctor's office. I thought it odd, but I didn't dwell on the fact I had not heard from the doctor. The day for my appointment with Dr. Hoagland arrived, and because the fluid from the drainage tubes had drastically diminished, I knew I would have the pesky plastic things removed. Tom was already at work in town, so my dear friends from down the street, Reta and Linda, came by to drive me into Louisville. Tom said he would meet me at the doctor's office. The three of us yucked it up all the way into town and carried our laughter into the waiting room. Tom was waiting and mentioned he had asked Joel to join us. That was interesting, but I just thought, *Isn't that nice!*

I was called back to the examination room. While Tom and I waited in the small sterile cell, me perched atop the table and Tom sitting beside me, I nonchalantly commented I was perplexed no one had called with lab results. Tom cocked his head to the side and looking very puzzled replied, "Judy, they would have called if it was good news." There it was again, the slap in the face. The pronouncement meant I wasn't on my A game. I, the one with the gift of discernment, had slipped up again. I hadn't sensed at all that the absence of a phone call meant something was obviously amiss. Had I lost my gift? I sat there baffled. Then I realized why Tom had invited Joel to join us.

Dr. Hoagland swept into the room and cheerfully began removing the bandages. I had been worried that removing the tube might be painful, but with dexterity, he pulled it out and cleaned me up. He left, allowing me to dress, and said he would return in a few minutes to talk to me about the lab reports. I asked him if it would be okay to have our son in the room for the conversation, and he wholeheartedly approved. The nurse escorted Joel back to our room, and he sat on my side opposite Tom. Dr. Hoagland returned with a piece of paper in his hand, pulled up a chair, positioning himself at my feet. He interpreted the medical jargon that said the sentinel nodes were the only two affected by the cancer. That was good!

Then he read the outer-parameter-tissue report. At that point, everything got complicated, and the room began to spin. Remember, all along we thought we were dealing with a cancer the size of the tip of my pinky finger. Not so, said Dr. Hoagland. There were tendrils or streams of cancer extending to a radius the size of a lemon. The pathology report indicated every layer of tissue going to the outer limits had traces of cancer. Finally, he admitted, "Judy, I can't be certain I got it all." I heard what he said, but I was struggling to comprehend what it meant. I felt my eyes cross, and my heart reached a beating point that nearly exploded out of my chest. I heard the doctor add, "It would not be advisable to go back and do another lumpectomy."

"What does it mean?"

From the expression on his face, I could tell it hurt him terribly to utter, "You need to consider a mastectomy." He added, "And, because you have a history of cancer in your left breast, for your peace of mind, you need to consider a mastectomy of that breast too."

The room was quiet but spinning at an ever increasing speed. I tried to breathe evenly, and I knew I should say something, but nothing would come out of my mouth. I glanced down at Tom, and he was mute; his eyes lowered. Joel chimed in, "If the area affected is so large, why didn't you catch it six months ago?"

Gently Dr. Hoagland diagrammed the progression of the cancer, showing how it wasn't a fully defined tumor, but small etchings that couldn't be seen until they started to overlap and cluster together. Joel continued asking questions. He was the voice of reason in the midst of the madness, the only one of us who could focus on what needed to be discussed. It turned out he was our lifesaver. If he hadn't been there we would have failed to ask appropriate questions just because the heavy cloud of numbness swirled and descended like a wet blanket over our souls.

Reta and Linda where waiting, unsuspecting of all that had just transpired. We walked out, and they looked at us, smiling, expecting a continuation of the merriment prior to my appointment. I'm sure they immediately saw that the mirth had vanished, and they questioned if everything was okay. I waited until we got to the hallway to tell them the news. We walked to the car and as soon as we got in and headed for Shelbyville, I looked at my dear friends and said,

"Listen, I can be morose or I can be spiritual, but I'm not going to be either. I'm telling you I'm counting on the two of you to make me laugh over the next few months. Do you hear me?" They nervously agreed.

I continued, "Reta, you have a tendency to send me questionable jokes and stories through e-mail, but I don't care anymore. Send them on."

Reta gaffed aloud, "Me? I send you questionable jokes?"

"Yes, you do, and you know you do, but it's okay for now. I'll tell you when to rein it in." Some of you cringed at my telling Reta to send on the jokes. Don't worry. It was just my way of dealing with the situation at hand. I hadn't abandoned my walk with the Lord. Quite the opposite. I was about to enter into the closest relationship with my Father that I'd ever had.

I had no idea until later, but Linda was to face her own mammogram the following day and would ultimately have to follow me down the much traveled road of breast surgery.

I hadn't bargained for this. Actually, I hadn't bargained for any of this! We had one week to discuss, pray, and then give the doctor our decision. Tom was to have attended a work-related meeting that evening, but as we left the office he called his boss and told him he wouldn't be able to make it. We had a nice, leisurely, scrumptious meal left by Reta and Linda. And then we talked.

VISIONS OF DOLLY

☸

How does the saying go? When it rains, it pours? It was *raining* in October!

Tom tripped on an uneven sidewalk in front of his doctor's office and had a nasty fall. At first he thought he was going to be okay, but after returning to his work he realized there was more pain and swelling than should occur with just a sprain. I met him at the hospital where he found out he had broken his wrist. There I was waiting for the call from Dr. Hoagland, so I could verify our decision to go ahead with the bilateral mastectomy, and Tom was stretched out on a table in the emergency room. Could it get any more weird?

My phone rang, and the office nurse set me up for the operation on Thursday, October 23. Depending on my recovery and the start of chemo treatments, she assured me there may be time for us to go to New Jersey in November to see Maia.

In the meantime, Joel made arrangements to fly to Philadelphia a few days after Maia's birth, so he could help with Gideon, freeing Kenny and Trina to concentrate on Maia's care.

Surgery day arrived, and it was routine. In addition to Joel and Toby, our youngest son, Micah, joined in the wait. The first thing Dr. Hoagland said to me following the operation was, "I've left plenty of extra skin so the plastic surgeon will have extra tissue to work with." In the hubbub of decisions that were made to proceed with surgery, I had forgotten to tell him I had decided not to have reconstruction. Oh, well, I didn't think it would make any difference. Time would prove that assumption to be wrong.

Most often, women undergoing mastectomies are required by their insurance carrier to be released from the hospital the same day. In other words, they consider it an outpatient procedure. I was blessed to stay overnight. When it was time for me to be discharged, my favorite nurse, Melanie, took me into the bathroom to change out of the hospital gown. I had been given a beautiful camisole to wear under my "going-away" clothes. Made of a soft cotton flannel with lace trim, the Soft-Tee® was invented by a lady who felt self-conscious leaving the hospital after her surgery. The undergarment had little pockets for the drainage tubes, and fluffy little pillows of cotton down could be inserted into Velcro taped openings where the breasts would normally appear. Melanie helped me slip the flannel-like tee over my head, and she positioned the drainage bulbs into the little pockets. She took the pillows of fluff and tucked them into place. I put on my button-down top and looked at myself in the mirror. We burst into laughter, for there staring back at me was a Dolly Parton replica.

I lost count of the number of times we opened up the slits and pulled out the fluffy filler. Finally, we got my boobs "down to size." Even then, I felt more self-conscious with my pillowed form than I would have if nothing had been there at all.

MAMMARY MUSINGS

I must add a caveat here: For those of you who are easily offended by the talk of anything even slightly embarrassing, you might want to skip this chapter. I'm going to write about my relationship with my breasts. So put down the book, examine your heart, and if you decide you can't continue reading, I'll understand. Just go to the next chapter. It's okay.

After my surgery I wouldn't allow myself to look at my bandaged chest. Tom took note and called me out on it. I told him I just couldn't look yet. I guess I was in a state of denial. I don't know, but even when I returned home, I just did what I had to do to change the drainage bulbs and chose not to look in the mirror at my bare self. The doctor had told us Tom and I could remove the bandages on our own, or we could wait and have him do it when he took out the tubes. I decided it would be good to have the doctor do the job.

The first time I stepped out of the shower following the removal of the bandages, I was in a state of shock. The image staring back at me was not the image I had expected. A few years earlier, I had seen a picture in a magazine of a woman who had both breasts removed; she didn't look like this. Her torso was flat from the shoulders down to her waist. That isn't at all what I saw. I hadn't taken into consideration the spare tire wrapped around my middle. Not only that, but the doctors had taken much more tissue than I was expecting. It was not a flat chest. It was a concave chest. Did they have to take so much? I wilted into convulsions of tears streaming down my cheeks. This was not what I thought it would be.

I've always had a love-hate relationship with my breasts. When I first started developing, I was very shy about my body. I didn't mature like some of my friends, and I found I was left "wanting" in size and abundance, resembling Olive Oyl, and requiring the smallest size bras on the market. It wasn't until my 50s or 60s that additional weight to my hips also granted me a little bit more volume on top. In the meantime, I endured the lack of endowment by stuffing tissue in my bra cups to fill them out.

In my youth, most bras were pointed. Even with the extra "help" crammed inside, if I got a snug enough hug from a friend, the points would dent in permanently, leaving my form to look like I'd been in a fender bender. You can't imagine my joy when makers of undergarments came up with the brilliant idea to make padded bras. Not only could I abandon using tissues, which had a tendency to creep up and spill out at the oddest times, but the prefab underwear made me look downright normal.

It is just too bad the luxury shape shifter wasn't invented until after my senior trip. (Yes, I go back that far!) In those "golden" days, high-school seniors went on class trips. My school, Lakeside, in Hot Springs, Arkansas, went to the Gulf of Mexico. Our first stop was Pensacola, Florida. I shared a room with several other girls, and the minute we got to our motel, we changed into our swim suits. Mine was brand new, black, and had plenty of room in the bust area for an average-size figure to fill it out. Because the built-in bra was rigid, I looked very well endowed. I strutted to the beach with my other classmates, and we plunged into the foaming surf. The first wave hit me full on, but when the tide ebbed, so did my swim suit. I was left standing in thigh-deep water with the top half of my suit floating down around my waist. I was aghast with horror. My arms and hands never moved so fast to pull up the straps. Most of the seniors got an eyeful during the time it took to restore my dignity.

During the summer break between my sophomore and junior years in college, I made a trip with a friend to Springfield, Missouri, for a Chi Alpha conference. The last night of the meeting, I met a nice young man. Tom Gerdis was his name. We started writing, and in the fall of 1966 he came to Hot Springs to visit over Thanksgiving weekend. My father was the administrator of a children's home, and Tom had met my parents when he visited the area a year earlier to write an article about the children and the ministry of the home.

Tom let me decide what we would do for our first date. Since the children's home was located outside Hot Springs, I decided I would take him into town via the most scenic route, a country road that would take us out by Lake Hamilton. After a meal of fried clams (my favorite at the time), we planned to go down Central Avenue and take in the action at one of the auction houses. We parked directly across from Bathhouse Row and the healing waters bubbled up from the ground in fountains of mist.

While we were in the auction house, a rain shower came through. I hadn't rolled up the window on the passenger side of the car, so when we returned to Tom's car after strolling up West Mountain, I realized the seat was wet, which required me to move to the center position. We headed for home down Malvern Avenue, and the skies opened up with a downpour making it impossible to see to drive even with the wipers going full speed. Because the road had "lips" on the edge, Tom kept going over the side, almost losing control of the vehicle. Finally, because of the danger, he pulled over to the side in a parking lot to wait for the deluge to stop. During this lull, Tom mentioned (ever so nonchalantly) his mother had told him he would never meet someone who possessed all the attributes he wanted in a wife. Then he asked if I wanted to hear what those were? I was captive in a car, a hurricane was raging outside, and I had no way to escape. Curious about what might be on his list, I replied, "Sure."

Ten items were on his list. Of the few I can remember were that she had to be a committed Christian (check), she couldn't be too much taller or shorter than he (check), she had to be able to type (check – and later learned that meant

I would be typing his thesis and dissertation), she had to have a heart for hospitality (check), and the last item was she couldn't be too "buxom." I was floored! Having lived in the South for 10 years, it was understood a gentleman would not even broach such a subject with a lady! *Dumbfounded* was the perfect word to describe what was churning inside. I never! (CHECK!)

I have to acknowledge right here and right now . . . he lied!

I married him despite his "list," and over the years it has become quite apparent, as with all men, form precedes function, not vice versa. Recently, Tom tried to explain to me that our conversation that dark and stormy night was not what I had assumed, and the reason for his comment was that he felt women well endowed tended to be vain.

As they were growing up, even my children noticed something wasn't quite right with their mother. Once when Trina and Joel were youngsters, they came to me with brows furrowed and asked, "Why don't you have a line, Mom?" A

line? What could they be referring to? A *line*?

"What are you talking about?"

"You know, a line," Trina quipped.

Joel added, "Like Nancy! A line like Nancy has."

I thought for a few minutes, before it hit me. Nancy

had abundant breasts! She had cleavage! They were talking

about *cleavage*! How does one explain such disadvantages

to five- and nine-year-old children? I had been overcompen-

sating for my lack of a "line" for many years by squeezing

my arms together when necessary, which created the sem-

blance of a "line" when it was called for.

After my mastectomy, I was directed to visit The Spe-

cial Lady, a shop catering to women facing and experiencing

mastectomies. I dropped by for a visit without knowing the

owner preferred her customers to have appointments so pri-

vacy could be provided to those requiring her services. For-

tunately, no one else was in the shop during my first visit. The owner was more than accommodating, showing me around her shop and explaining all my options. She pulled out prosthetic after prosthetic and showcased them on the checkout counter. There were all different shapes and sizes ranging from affordable to unbelievably expensive. The latest on the market looked and felt like the real thing and had a sticky backing with little suction bumps that latched onto the skin and held them tight, giving the wearer the option to wear a bra or not. The bras had little pockets that held the fake boobs in place. The sales lady placed one in my hand, and I couldn't stop stroking the smooth surface. It was ridiculous! These things were amazingly life like. I knew, as I kept petting the breast in my hand, if anyone walked through the door, I would certainly look like a fool. However, I kept the prosthetic in my hand and told the lady, "I think I'll buy one of the small ones for my husband to keep in his pocket." She keeled over in laughter.

When I had healed enough that wearing a bra wouldn't chafe, I returned to the shop for a proper fitting. I started out with the cup size I had been wearing at the time I had been diagnosed with breast cancer. I turned to look in the mirror and stood sideways admiring my silhouette. The owner asked what I thought. I turned to her and with my right thumb upright; I raised it skyward. "Oh, you want it to be a little larger?"

"Yes", I whispered.

She returned with a larger size and slipped them into the mesh pocket. I turned and looked again. It dawned on me I could finally be any size I wanted. Any size at all. I raised my thumb again, pointing to the ceiling. "Bigger?" she asked.

"Yes," I nodded.

So I am now an ample size. I have an $800 "line." OK, I definitely don't have a "line" these days, but they are plush and lush even though from time to time I sorely miss what God gave me. They weigh a pound and a half apiece. Three pounds! So I gladly take that into consideration when I step on the scales, deducting the amount to come up with my "real" weight. I just wish the doctors would take that into account as well when I have check-ups. I've tried to wear the suctioned pieces without the benefit of a bra, but just as it was in the days of my youth, they wouldn't stick. Some things never change.

BIRTH DAY

October 29, 2008. Maia's birthday had arrived. Glynnis Ballou, a long-time friend from our days living in Kansas, had traveled to Shelbyville from Shepherdsville, Kentucky, to stay with me for a few days. I was glad she would be waiting with me for the news just in case anything went wrong with the delivery and Maia's care afterward.

Trina called at 8:00 AM. They were getting ready to wheel her back to the operating room. She just wanted to check in and talk to her momma before the big event. I could tell she was a little on edge. So I said, "Do you want to laugh a little bit?" She said that would be terrific. So I told her I had dreamed she had called, crying, "Oh, mom, Maia isn't a girl at all. I had a boy! What are we going to do with all those pink dresses?"

In an effort to calm her, I said, "Oh, don't worry, Honey. Maybe Joel and Toby will have a girl, and they can use all the little girl outfits."

"But what are we going to name him? We weren't planning for this!"

"Just a minute. Let me pray about it. I'm sure the Lord will give me a name. Hold on."

In my dream I returned to the phone a few minutes later, "I've got it! The Lord wants you to name him Hans Zachariah!"

Trina started belly laughing. I think she laughed all the way into delivery.

At 10:30, I told Glynnis, "I'm starting to worry." At that precise moment, the phone rang, and I could hear Trina's voice so clear, she sounded like she was in the next room.

Maia was born at 9:32 AM, much later than they had thought because she was scrunched way up high in the birth canal and scar tissue from Gideon's birth had made it difficult for the doctors to do their job. She had a healthy cry, her lungs filled with air. She weighed 6 pounds, 5 ounces with blue eyes and blonde hair.

Maia's Apgar score was an 8.9 of a possible 10. Her coloring was pink with no signs of heart distress. When she cried uncontrollably during the testing, Kenny started singing to her, and she calmed right down. She had a tube in her belly button, which had been inserted for the tests to come, and an echo cardiogram would be performed by day's end. Trina said the delivery room attendants kept telling her how calm she appeared. She said she was more peaceful than she had ever been in her life.

From 1957 to 1968, my dad was administrator of Hillcrest Children's Home in Hot Springs, Arkansas. Early in 2008, I reconnected with many of the "children" who had been there during the time we lived on campus. One of the

ladies from that era sent the following poem.

The Miracle Arrival of Princess Maia Elizabeth Suther-

land

Weighing in at 6 lbs. 5 oz., on October 29, at 9:32 AM,

In the year 2008,

A new little Princess made her arrival . . .

On GOD's appointed date.

All wrapped up in Buttons and Bows,
She begins her Earthly journey.
Her beautiful sounds bring tears of joy.
She smells of Milk and Honey.

Inside her . . . lies . . . the Hope of the Future,
And ALL the Wisdom of the Ages.
God gives each one of us . . . a Book.
It's up to us . . . to fill the pages.

I hope your Pages are filled with Joy, Little Maia,
And every kind of pleasure.
I hope that all your dreams come true,
And your pockets are filled with treasure.

May you face each challenge in your life
As your "nana," Judy, would . . . With Courage, Strength
and Honor.
May you never cease to see the Good in ALL,
Nor lose your sense of Wonder.

Don't worry. Live Simply. Speak kindly, little Maia.
Always give others a second chance.
And if you have the choice to sit on the sidelines . . .
Or DANCE with LIFE,
I certainly hope you DANCE. [2]

Love,
Lil Walter
October 29, 2008

BLOOD, SWEAT AND TEARS

❀

The day following Maia's birth, her condition deteriorated. She had to have a valvuloplasty procedure, which was successful; however, when doctors tried to use her right femoral artery, they couldn't lace the line. They abandoned her right leg and used her left. She made it out of surgery but lost a lot of blood. Her temperature fell, and no matter what the team did, it wouldn't budge. They couldn't get a pulse in her right leg, and the decision was made to give her a blood transfusion later in the evening.

When Trina called to give me the update on Maia, I just happened to be in an ultrasound room with our son, Joel, and his pregnant wife, Toby. Holding the phone away from my ear and extending it toward the ultrasound technician, Trina heard, "Can you see what that is?We all shouted, "It's a boy!" Toby's due date would be in March. So, Ethan would have a little brother.

Joel, an individual contractor, had parked his Jeep, with his tool trailer in tow, behind Hooters (no joke) because there weren't any parking spaces at the nearby Medical Towers building. After the ultrasound, he hopped in his vehicle and took off to run some errands. The first time he had to turn right, he was shocked to see the trailer doors swing out to the curb. He pulled to the side of the street and went back to secure the lock. He then realized that while he was inside finding out his second child would be a boy, someone had broken the padlock on his trailer and stolen some of his most expensive tools. What a let down! He spent the rest of the afternoon at the police station and the insurance company filing reports. In spite of his disappointment, he had a good attitude and told me, "Mom, I know one person saw what happened and that was God."

Although Maia improved steadily, she had to have two blood transfusions, but her vital signs leveled out.

I had the appointment with Dr. Hoagland to remove my bandages. He gave us permission to travel to New Jersey the week of November 9, which was perfect timing, so we could be there when Joel had to return to Louisville. I couldn't fly due to the pressurized cabin, so we planned to drive and cut the 13-hour trip in half by staying with friends in West Virginia. My first visit with the oncologist was scheduled for November 17· and Tom was to have his cast removed November 19. Yes, the "window of opportunity" we had prayed for did open up. We just couldn't wait to wrap our arms around our New Jersey family and especially little "ladybug," Maia.

Trina had planned to decorate Maia's nursery with a ladybug theme, so Maia became known as Ladybug early on in her development. That was fine with me, as I have long applied nicknames to my grandchildren. Gideon would get a kick out of my calling him Sweet Pea and Snicker-doodle.

Sunday, November 2, I received a call from Trina, "Guess who we have with us in the car?"

"I bet you have Snookums, Sweet Pea, and Snicker-doodle with you!"

The call was on speaker phone, and I heard Gideon yell out, "That's me!"

I talked with him for a few minutes, and he was very excited to be traveling to Pennsylvania to see his baby sister for the first time. He chattered about all his grandiose plans for Maia.

The Children's Hospital of Philadelphia is an amazing facility, designed specifically for the needs of children and their parents and families. They think of everything, including a nap room where siblings and other members of their patients' families can rest and regain their strength.

There are playrooms and snack bars for the youngsters and computer labs for e-mail messages or games.

When they checked into the Ronald McDonald House (RMH) for the night, Trina discovered they were staying in the original RMH. It's a gracious old mansion with amenities galore and designed for every need a family might encounter while caring for a sick child.

On Monday, Trina and Kenny were told Maia would be down graded from ICCU to CCU, which gave them hope she would get to go home sooner. The key factors for her early release would be the further closing of her ductus and her oxygen level stabilizing at 85 percent or higher.

In Shelbyville, I was preparing to have the drainage tubes removed. Most of my residual pain stemmed from those tubes, so I was excited to have the procedure done and over. The sooner I could get them out, the sooner we could leave for New Jersey. In the meantime, friends were lavishing us with wonderful meals, flowers, cards, letters, and phone calls.

Tuesday, November 4, our family was told Maia would be released from the hospital in the afternoon. It was decided Kenny would get mother and baby settled into the RMH, and he would take Gideon on home to New Jersey. Trina and Joel would take Maia home after Joel's arrival the next day. That was the plan, anyway. This early release came as a surprise since an echo cardiogram had not been performed since the Saturday before, at which point Maia's ductus was still open. Kenny ran out to buy a car seat and other baby supplies, and both Trina and Kenny had to take a CPR class so they would be prepared should an emergency require them to give their baby immediate care.

Right before her release, the hospital completed the echo cardiogram, and it showed the ductus was wide open. Unfortunately, this forced Maia's discharge to be postponed at the last minute. Bummer! It was a mixed bag of emotions, with frustration at the top of the list. At the same time, it was also confirmation the angst they had been feeling about going home early was well founded. Joel arrived and drove with Gideon to take Kenny back to New Jersey, so he could return to work. Then Joel was to turn around and go back to Philadelphia for the rest of the week. In the meantime, they hooked Maia up to additional oxygen, which could help to close the ductus.

Joel's job for the next several days would be to make sure Gideon was entertained. He was perfect for the job. Having a little boy, Ethan, at home and another on the way, meant he was willing to stand on his head if necessary to see that this four year old didn't get bored. Gideon can be an entertainer on his own, bursting into song at the drop of a hat and telling his own made-up stories at will. In the car on the way back to Philly, Joel and Gideon had the following conversation:

Joel: "Have you had any sushi lately?" (Gideon's favorite food since age 2.)

Gideon: "No. I haven't had any sushi in a long time."

Joel: "Why not?"

Gideon: "I don't know, but I had a lot of sushi in 'Tucky (his word for Kentucky)."

Joel: "Really?"

Gideon: "Yes. Gamma Judy got me sushi again, and again, and again, and again, and again, and again, and again, and again!"

Five days later, Tom and I arrived in Lakewood. Kenny had driven up to CHOP to relieve Trina for the weekend, and Joel had brought Trina and Gideon home, so they could have some much needed rest. We went to church Sunday, then we made our way back to the hospital for our watch and to let Kenny return to work.

The doctors were giving the ductus in Maia's heart one day to close. I sent out an e-mail plea for everyone to pray, figuring if God could make the world in six days, He could surely close a little hole in a precious little heart in one. If the hole didn't show signs of closing, the surgeons talked about adding a shunt in an open-heart procedure. I will never forget walking into the hospital room with baby Maia hooked up to all the tubes and machines. She looked so helpless and my heart broke as I neared her bedside railing. Oh, how small, yet beautiful, and absolutely precious. I couldn't hold back my tears. I just kept thanking God we could be there to touch and caress her soft, rosy cheeks and whisper sweet words of love and encouragement into her ear. It was a hassle, but we lifted her and held her close. Her heart rate and oxygen levels would actually improve when we wrapped our arms around her fragile body.

As the days progressed the doctors waffled on what to do. They could either keep Maia in the hospital and do open-chest surgery or let her go home. Her oxygen levels fluctuated, and her hemoglobin was a tad low. I was handling the routine well, my own healing occurring a smidgeon at a time. Being with my grandchildren made me feel like I was on top of the world.

BITTERSWEET
HOMECOMING DAY

✸

We were thrilled to get the go-ahead to check Maia out of the hospital and drive her home to New Jersey Thursday, November 14. Numerous tests were run, and doctor consultations were held before they would allow us to leave. Providentially, Kenny was in Philly at the time of the final okay, so he got to join us in the momentous occasion. He helped us clean out the room at the Ronald McDonald House, do the laundry, and load up the cars. All the waiting made it a long tiring day. During the late afternoon, an alarm went off in the unit, and I thought it must be a practice fire drill since the nurses came to Maia's pod and closed off the glass doors. I watched as they scurried

back and forth and expected them to return to their normal

routine, opening the partitions and letting in fresh air. It took

forever. I couldn't imagine what the hold up might be. When

Kenny arrived at the unit he came in from the left hallway

instead of the right as he normally had. He looked very

somber and with a serious, sad countenance, he told Trina

he thought maybe one of Maia's original roommates might

have died in the next unit. It wasn't a fire drill after all. It had

been a Code Blue.

His name was Carson,* and he had been in the NICU 10

weeks. His parents lived in West Virginia and, because of

their jobs, could come to visit him only on weekends. I just

couldn't imagine what it must have been like for his mother

to receive the phone call that afternoon that her baby son had

died. We were rejoicing we could take Maia home, and they

would have to make the sad, long journey to Philadelphia

to take their child home to be buried. It broke our hearts. I walked past what had been Carson's pod as we exited the NICU for home, and the nurses were carefully folding and putting away the blankets and straightening the lines that had once brought life to a little boy's body. They were wiping away their tears, and several of my own fell down my face and dropped from my chin as well.

The hospital sent a Pulse Ox machine with us so we could check Maia's pulse rate and oxygen levels. She seemed to settle in well to her new routine, but all of us kept hovering over her cradle to see if she was breathing and to make sure her color was pink, not blue.

Two days later, I accompanied Trina to Maia's first appointment with the pediatric cardiologist. She ran her own tests on Maia and told us the ductus had closed a little more and now stood at 1.9 mm, but she saw other problems with the aorta valve and the bicuspids, which are located on the left side of her heart. This was a big surprise to Trina as no one at CHOP had mentioned other defects. Maia would be seeing her cardiologist every week until the ductus closed, then every month for the first year of her life. She made it very clear Maia was not out of the woods. Two arterial flaps were fused together, so the next six months would be critical in determining future treatment.

Gideon was all excited about returning to school that Friday. It would be show-and-tell day, and I thought he would want to bring Maia. However, he was planning on showing off his two new animated transformers. Just like a little brother, wouldn't you say? Showing off Maia would come another day. While Gideon prepared for show-and-tell, Tom and I prepared to return to Kentucky. We wondered if the skies would clear up so our trip would be on dry roads. It had been wet and blustery for two days. My first appointment with the oncologist would be the next Monday. The last of my staples were coming out Tuesday, and Tom would have his cast removed Wednesday. A busy week was ahead of us.

MIRACLE ON I-64

§

After our trip home to Kentucky, I logged on to the Internet to check e-mail and saw note after note from friends saying they would be praying for our journey. I started to cry. I knew as I read each message the power of prayer had been demonstrated in a miraculous way.

We left Lakewood around 10:00 in the morning. When we neared Rocky Gap Resort in Maryland where we had thought we might stay the night, it was still too early in the day to stop, and Tom decided we should just keep heading west. The rain that had plagued us in New Jersey was still descending, and the skies were heavy with dark clouds. As the sun set, it became more difficult to see the road. I was so glad we were driving my car because it was heavy and clung to the road a little better than Tom's.

Around 8:00 pm., we neared the first exits for Huntington, West Virginia, on I-64. We noticed a big, red, flatbed semi tractor-trailer start to pull along the driver's side of the car. We approached a hill, and the truck slowed, so Tom pulled slightly ahead. I heard the semi's engine rev up, as though the driver was gunning to pass. Suddenly we were hit. The noise was deafening. Tom grabbed the wheel and brought the fish-tailing car under control. We both looked over to our left at the same time and saw the red monster moving into our lane again. I started yelling, "He's coming over! He's coming over!" (Tom says he will never forget the way I screamed out. I guess I was visualizing what would happen if a semi were to drive us off the road.)

Tom hit the shoulder of the highway and came to a screeching halt. The truck sailed on by. At first, we thought about moving into traffic to try and run him down, so we could get some identification from the trailer, but he was long gone — disappearing into the heavy traffic, the rain, and the night. Both of us just sat there breathing in deep gasps of air and trying to calm ourselves. I dialed 911 on my cell phone and explained what had just happened. A highway patrolman was dispatched. It didn't take long for the officer to arrive, but the wait seemed like an eternity. He shined his flashlight into the car, and asked if we were okay. Of course we were, we explained, but we were a bit unsettled. He told us he understood.

Tom went with the patrolman to the cruiser so they could file a report. As I waited in the car, I glanced up the road and saw a bridge abutment no more than 200 feet ahead of us. *My, my*, I thought, *if the truck had hit us just a few feet farther from where we were, there wouldn't have been any space to get out of the way.* We would have been crushed.

I tried calling Trina, but no one answered, so I called Joel. Toby answered and when we told her what had happened, she started praising the Lord. She and Ethan had just prayed for our safety 15 minutes before the accident occurred. Then my phone rang, and it was Kenny apologizing because he hadn't answered earlier. They were having devotions with Gideon and praying for our safety. We felt the Lord's presence so strong, and we were so grateful for his protection. We were thankful we were driving a heavy car with new tires, as anything lighter would have probably gone airborne. Amazingly, we didn't hydroplane, which we probably would have done if the rain had been heavier. What is most unbelievable is after being hit we thought the whole left side of the car likely was scraped, mangled and dented. It wasn't. We found only one small dented area where the driver's door and the passenger door meet. I decided I wouldn't even get it repaired right away. It would serve as a reminder that prayers are powerful and God's traveling mercies, divine.

PART II
STORMY WEATHER
❂

PLAN OF ACTION

I had my first oncology appointment at the treatment center. Tom accompanied me but had to leave before the doctor appeared. I learned my initial report set the cancer at Stage II. After the lumpectomy and mastectomy, the medical team in charge of my treatments had upgraded it to a Stage III since cancer cells were found in the perimeter and the two sentinel nodes. For that reason, the doctor insisted the wisest course would be radiation following the chemo treatments. I had thought I would skip radiation altogether. This was a surprise turn in the road.

They penciled me in for an educational DVD to help me more fully understand the chemo process. A CAT scan, PET scan, and MRI were also scheduled. My first chemotherapy session would be the following Tuesday.

I didn't want Tom to have to be away from his work for the chemotherapy treatments. He could take me to the early morning appointments, but I would need someone to drive me home to Shelbyville, 20 miles away. The call went out for volunteers, and I was amazed at all who signed on for chauffeur duty.

Donna Gunnoe accompanied me to the orientation session. One of the nurse technicians walked us through the treatment room where 20 or more recliner chairs and 10 or more beds were lined up in rows. Some were against the walls, some in curtained-off alcoves and tiny rooms for privacy. It was late in the day, but there were still a few patients either dozing or visiting with friends as the chemo drips flowed down from the vials hanging precariously above their heads. This was where I would be camping out over the next six months.

The nurse gave us the nickel tour, pointing out the snack bar and the refrigerator containing soft drinks, juices, and water. Then we walked through a small side door into a conference room. After trying unsuccessfully to get the DVD to play, she gave us a verbal run down of what I could expect. Using several sheets of paper, she showed that the first four treatments would be of one "cocktail" variety, and the last four would be another. The first four would probably cause the nausea often associated with chemotherapy, and the last four would have a myriad different symptoms. Each cocktail plan had a long list of side effects, which I was expected to sign off on toward the bottom of the page. The list began with minor symptoms, and all of them ended with "death." After going over page after page, my eyes started crossing, and looking back, I realize I didn't pay attention as well as I should have. After all, . . . death? Naw, that wasn't going to happen to me.

As Donna and I entered the elevator to descend to the lobby, she looked at me wide eyed, "Did you know about all those side effects?" I assured her I did, but most of what I had just heard and read went in one ear and out the other. I was determined to be different. I wouldn't succumb to all the fears and all those side effects. After all, I had a job I was intent on keeping. If I came down with everything on the list, there would be no way I could continue working.

I had told my employer I had never missed a day of work when I had cancer 13 years earlier, and I planned not to miss many days this time either. They all laughed because they knew what was ahead. Every member of my employer's family had experienced cancer. They knew but couldn't tell me all I would be facing in the coming months. I would have to go through my own storm. They did tell me not to worry about my job, adding I was free to go to work when I felt like it and free to remain home when I didn't. That was to prove to be one of the greatest blessings and dearest gifts I could

receive.

GOING BACK TO BEFORE
✹

Tuesday of Thanksgiving week Tom and I got to the treatment center on the fifth floor of the medical building at 8:40 AM. I was rushed back to the lab immediately, and I thought, *This is a good sign. Maybe I'll be able to start my treatment early.* Tom decided to stay with me until we received all the scan reports and for the first chemo drip to begin.

I had wanted to have a port installed so that inserting needles in my hand and arm would be unnecessary, but Dr. Hoagland couldn't find the time on his surgery schedule to get the port implanted. Since I had good veins in my left hand and arm, I didn't think the port would make a difference. Because the lymph nodes had been removed, I couldn't have any needles or blood pressure cuffs administered on my right side.

We waited in the examination room for more than an hour and a half. So much for expediting the whole process! Finally the oncologist was able to get to us. He had all my recent scans available and all were normal. (Big sigh of relief.) The only thing causing him pause was my low white count. He couldn't quite figure out why my white cells would be so low since I hadn't started treatments yet. This proved to be an indication of things to come.

Tom had to leave, and I made my way to the treatment waiting room on my own. I sat across from a lady I had seen receiving chemo during my tour the previous week. She wore a baseball cap over her bald head and appeared quite friendly, so I ventured a conversation.

"How long have you been receiving treatments?" I asked.

"Oh, let's see," she said. "I guess in January it will be one year."

She continued, "I should have known. My mother had breast cancer at 62, and I'm 52. I've had precancerous cells for many years, and the doctors were keeping an eye on them, but, you know, things just got away from us."

They called her name, and she excused herself. I was called right after she left and told to pick out a recliner. Most were filled, but I found one by a window. As I was settling myself in for the long haul, I heard someone say, "Is Judy Gerdis back here?"

It was my friend Donna Gunnoe. I was so happy to see her, I almost cried. I settled in, and Donna wrapped a new pink blanket she had made around my legs. It had the breast cancer awareness ribbons in the design. At first I thought it would be too warm for me, but as the cocktail penetrated my body I shivered with an icy cold that radiated from my hands and arms to my shoulders.

All those who worked with me that day had also treated my friend, Mary. They spoke so lovingly of her and her husband, Doug. Was I sitting in one of the chairs where Mary waged her valiant fight?

I had drugs added to my IV before the big stuff arrived. Then my nurse, Missy, robed up, dropped a plastic shield over her face, and donned a mouth mask and heavy gloves before administering the chemo. I asked if the rest of us shouldn't have the same protection, and she just smiled. I guess not.

I'm not sure when Donna left. I can't remember. The relaxation drugs must have clicked in. I do remember talking to a family across from me. The mother had colon cancer, and she only had two more treatments to go. She was a very pretty lady who kept adjusting her wig. Her teenage son sat nearby, and her parents crowded around her feet. Originally from New Jersey and now living in Florida, they were planning on a happy Thanksgiving in Kentucky.

I thought I would be out of the office by 10:00 or 11:00, but the nurse didn't take the tubes from my hand until 1:15. I called Peggy Campbell (a "pew mate" from church) who lived close by and had volunteered to pick me up. When she found out I hadn't had anything to eat since 7:00 that morning, she took me for a sandwich, and then she drove me home. The rest of the day and on into the next, I waited for the side effects to set in. I was a little shaky and weak, but it wasn't at all bad.

Then Thanksgiving morning, at precisely 4:00, I awoke to nausea that wouldn't go away. I finally got up at 5:00 and took my first pill to try to combat the waves of queasiness washing over me. I went back to bed, but the rest of the day I slid in and out of "never-never land." I had planned for a simple meal at our home just in case: paper plates, cups, and a store-bought honey ham. Our family and guests would bring all the side dishes, and friends had already brought us several desserts. Once the party got started, I sat and observed, trying not to stir too much. By 8:00 in the evening, the nausea had subsided a bit, but then a low headache, body aches and weakness plagued me on into Friday.

This is a little taste of what is ahead for me I thought. Chemo had been a mystery until then. As I climbed the stairs to go to bed, I glanced over at Tom at the computer and said, "I want to go back."

"Go back where?" he asked.

"I want to go back to before," I said.

I kept thinking about Jesus, knowing what was before him, asking the Father, "Hey, if you don't mind, and if you can work it out, I'd rather not go through this. Okay?" (My paraphrase.)

Then the other thoughts and fears set in: What did I do to acquire this cancer? Was it my hairspray? Maybe the gel I use to make my hair shine? Could it have been the ointment I put on my knee to stop the arthritic pain? Or maybe it was dying my hair auburn. It went on and on. All the "what ifs"

tumbled through my head.

Yup, I just wanted to go back. I kept thinking, I'm ready

for a do over.

TELL ME IT ISN'T SO

❀

Throughout the year I wrote and e-mailed newsletters every few days or weeks, filling people in on my progress and the insights my cancer walk brought. However, one heartache I failed to mention actually turned into the greatest joy of our year.

The moment came Thursday evening after all the Thanksgiving dishes had been washed and put away, and all the family and guests had gone home. Our youngest son, Micah, was the only one remaining. He had come out to Shelbyville by himself that day, leaving Gina, his girlfriend of six years, to celebrate the holiday with her family in Louisville.

I thought it odd that Micah didn't seem to be in a hurry to join Gina, but stayed behind and settled in to watch some television with me in the family room while Tom checked his e-mails in the adjoining office. At one point, Micah leaned over to me and said, "Mom, I need to tell you something." What was it that immediately caused my heartbeat to increase and my sweat glands to overreact? Was it the way he lowered his voice? The way he gulped with hesitancy before saying, "Gina is pregnant." He went on, "She is 28 weeks and just found out. She didn't know."

A little voice in my head started screaming, "Why? Why? Why now? Couldn't this have come, oh say, *anytime* other than now?"

He continued, "Because she didn't know, the doctors are really concerned that all the medicine she has been taking for her lupus and her methadone treatments will have a negative effect on the baby."

I finally found my voice, "Micah, do you love Gina?"

"Yes."

"Do you want to marry her?"

"I'd love to, Mom, but because of all her debt and all my debt, I just can't go there right now."

"What do you plan to do?"

"We'll have the baby, but it is going to be rough. They will put Gina in the hospital until the birth. Then the baby will have to be there until they can wean it off the drugs."

The voice in my head continued to scream, "Why? Why? Why? Oh, God, I need you now! Help me! Help us all!"

"Well, Micah, you have to tell your father."

"I know. I know. Will you help me?"

I called into the next room, and Tom came and sat in the rocking chair across from us. With my heart in my mouth I said, "Micah has something he needs to tell you."

As Micah confessed his circumstances, I saw the look of disbelief cross Tom's face. We had been very concerned that

Gina was getting a regular dosage of methadone from the local clinic as part of their maintenance program.

When Micah finished, Tom looked at the carpet and sighed deeply, "Micah, we have always wanted the best for our children. I'm like all dads, I've had dreams for you. This is not what I dreamed."

At that, Micah's chest heaved, and with tears streaming down his cheeks he said, "I know, Dad. All my life, all I've ever wanted to do was make you and Mom proud of me, and I know this disappoints you. I'm so sorry. I'm so sorry." With that, both my men stood and hugged and cried in each others' arms.

The voice inside me kept screaming, "Oh, God, I don't know if I can go through all this. I knew it was going to be a difficult journey, this adventure you've called me to, but I didn't bargain for all this: Maia, my cancer, now this. Oh, God, hear me! I need you now more than I've ever needed you! Hear me, Lord. Hear my cry!"

Gina was hospitalized in December and remained there for two months as they lowered her methadone levels and prepared her to deliver the baby. We celebrated Christmas with them in the hospital and showered them with baby gifts. Kaya Francine was born January 21, 2009, and she was assigned to the NICU where she remained for another two months. At birth, she was immediately injected with Nalozone, a drug that counteracts any traces of narcotics in newborns and sends them into instant withdrawal. Doctors then prescribed the lowest dose of morphine required to alleviate her symptoms, and over the next several weeks the dose of morphine was reduced until it was no longer necessary. Because some babies experience withdrawal and others don't (known as abstinence syndrome), the protocol is to treat them all as if they will, to minimize their discomfort.

Kaya never exhibited any deficiencies in motor skills, and thrived until the day she was discharged from the hospital. She was the most precious baby I'd ever seen. With shocks of cold black hair streaked with blond, she looked

like a little rock star. She has become a rolly-polly fun-filled

ball of delight.'

BAD HAIR DAY
OR
MOMMA NEVER TOLD ME THERE WOULD BE DAYS LIKE THIS . . . BUT THE DOCTOR DID

☸

I was relaxing in our TV room recliner, but getting comfortable seemed impossible. "Why is my scalp so tender?" It felt like little needle pricks and itched like crazy. When I reached up to scratch, I felt nothing but pain. Then it dawned on me, "Oh, oh! Let's see . . . it has been precisely two weeks since my first chemo treatment, and the doctor said my hair would start falling out about two weeks later." Mmmm . . .

I went to sleep tossing and turning, trying to find the perfect spot to lay my head. It didn't matter. Every position hurt. I fully expected to find hair spread out over the pillow the next morning, but when I rose there wasn't any sign of hair left behind. I showered carefully, making sure when I washed my hair I didn't scrub, but when I rinsed out the shampoo and conditioner there was more hair than usual left in my hands. I decided to forgo the highlighting cream that added shine because I was afraid it would weigh down the follicles and speed up the exodus of my locks. Nevertheless, when I blew my mop dry, there was an abundance of auburn hair on the round brush bristles. I knew what was happening, yet I wanted to preserve every strand as long as I could. My hairdresser had told me my hair would probably not fall out in huge clumps because I'd been using a treatment that helped prevent excessive hair loss. She suggested, however, I not wait until I was left with a few strands here and there, rather I should call her any time night or day, and she would meet me at the salon and buzz it all off.

I had blood work and doctor's appointments the next day, and the wind had blown in gusty rain and even a little bit of snow. *Oh, oh,* I thought, *just maybe my hair would blow off my head, and that would save me from having it shaved away.*

All the blood was drawn, and I waited to see the doctor. He came into the examination room and said, "I'm very concerned about your white blood-cell count. Anything below 1,000 is dangerous, and yours is 140." I nearly fell off the table in shock! 140?

I was sent home and warned . . . "do not pass go," head straight to Shelbyville, and stay away from crowds! I was put on a powerful antibiotic, and the hospital was notified I would not be in the next day for the long awaited port installation.

More and more hair was coming out, but I just couldn't bring myself to call Cheryl, my hairdresser. Two more days passed, and I walked into the bathroom, ran my fingers through my hair, and large strands just fell away. There was a large bald spot near my crown, and as I put on my makeup I noticed hair falling without provocation into the sink and covering my shoulders. "Breathe deep. Don't let this get to you, Judy," I told myself. "You knew this was coming."

I called my neighbor down the street, Reta Stivers (the same Reta who had been with me when I received the cancer news.) She agreed to accompany me to my lab appointment, followed by a visit to the funeral home to express condolences at the death of a mutual friend, and then on to Changes Hair Salon in Jeffersontown. I had a premonition this was going to be an emotional day.

At the lab appointment, the report came back indicating my white-cell count was up to 2,000. Cha-ching! The port procedure was back on for the end of the week. We went on to the funeral home and spent time sharing with friends and family of the deceased. Then we were off to the guillotine! Fortunately, rather than my head, I was going to lose my hair.

When we arrived, I was surprised to see Toby, my daughter-in-law, and my 2 1/2-year-old grandson, Ethan. Following us through the door was Donna Gunnoe. I removed my coat, and Toby handed me a Victoria's Secret gift bag, "This is from Joel," she quipped.

I thought, *Why in the world would Joel be giving me a gift at this time and from Victoria's Secret, no less? Wait! Why would Joel ever give me a gift from Victoria's Secret?* I looked into the bag and saw a mass of dark brown hair that looked like some sort of dead animal. I was extremely puzzled and looked up at Toby for an explanation. She just smiled. I couldn't understand why Joel would buy me a wig when he knew I had already purchased one. This one looked gross! It wasn't even my color!

The door to the salon opened, and Joel walked in . . . BALD! He had neither hair on his head nor hair on his face. The beard and mustache he had been sporting were both gone. I said bald, didn't I? Let me take that back. He had tried, unsuccessfully, to shave his head. It was a botched job with ridges, bald spots, dents and puffs of hair here and there, but he was bald!

All the ladies in the salon erupted into shouts when Joel walked in. They yelled, screamed, clapped and laughed. It was an amazing sight. I told him I had thought the wad of hair in the bag resembled a dead animal, and he said, "That's what I was told when I was wearing it, Mom." Toby's mother and brother, Janet and Corey, stopped by the shop, as well. The time had come. Cheryl called my name. She was ready. I was not, but I didn't have a choice. Deep breaths . . . long deep breaths. It seemed like I had been taking long deep breaths a lot those days..

Cheryl turned the chair away from the mirror and started shaving from the back up to the crown of my head. I closed my eyes and prayed for strength. As I got closer and closer to being completely shaved, my friends and family could be heard saying, "Oh, Judy, you look so good! You have a beautifully shaped head. It isn't bad at all. Wait until you see yourself. You look so good!"

Cheryl turned the chair toward the mirror, and I saw my reflection. "You guys all need glasses!" I shrieked. I thought I was fully prepared for what I would see, but I doubt any woman would be ready to see herself completely bald. People were taking pictures, and there was a party atmosphere in the shop with posing, slaps on the back, congratulations and laughter. Cheryl started doing a repair job on Joel, and I quickly whipped out my wig, slapping it on my head.

All the way home Reta kept telling me how great I looked and offering words of encouragement. About half way to

Shelbyville she said, "Are we on I-64? What highway are we on?"

I looked at her and said, "You don't know what highway we're on, and you expect me to believe you when you tell me I look beautiful?" We laughed.

I didn't want to wear the wig at home all the time, only when I'd go out. That evening I tried on several little caps designed to keep my head warm, but the only thing that looked "cute" — which was very important for me — was a pink Green Bay Packers baseball cap a friend had donated to my cause. At bedtime I pulled on a pink stocking cap to keep my noggin snug. It wasn't bad — quite comfortable actually.

As dark descended, I pondered the day and came up with a new motto: I'd rather look good and feel bad than to feel good and look bad. I knew it was vanity at its best, but I figured I was entitled.

HAIR-RAISING TALES

Tom used to tell his friends, "I've slept with a blonde, brunette, and a red head, what more could a guy ask?" He meant, of course, I'd changed my hair color several times while we had been married.

A woman's hair has a strange place of honor, doesn't it? As a toddler my hair was a strawberry blonde and as kinky curly as a corkscrew. My mother had her hands full trying to style it in a way that didn't resemble a hornet's nest. Usually she did succeed in getting some Shirley Temple curls to cascade around my face. Because people often commented on my curls when I was a toddler, I was known to walk up to perfect strangers, pat my head and announce, "Pretty. Pretty."

As I aged, the frizz relaxed, and my hair darkened, but it still remained a source of frustration, especially during my high school and college years when the smooth page boy and flip were in style. Big gigantic rollers helped to soften the wiry bent of my wayward locks. Hair spray and Dippity-do came in handy, too. What really sealed the deal was discovering two forms of straightening once I went to college.

One trick was using permanent solution. I didn't believe it when someone told me to take the liquid portion out of the home-permanent box, mix it with water, and pour it over my hair. I was to comb or brush nonstop through the follicles, producing long, sleek styles even the hottest movie star would envy. I didn't care to let my hair grow long, mainly because the natural curl became even more unruly the longer my mane grew. Once or twice I experimented with the straight flip, and usually it worked well as long as

I had the teasing system in place. (Back in the dark ages we called it "ratting.")

Then, my roommate, Sandra Wall, and I discovered ironing our hair. Sandra always had longer hair than mine. She could do it. She also had a lot of natural curl and wave, so we would put up the ironing board in our dorm room, set the iron to medium, so we wouldn't singe away our tresses, and we would take turns ironing out all the wrinkles. Maybe this would last for a day, then we would have to do it all over again.

When the Afro style became popular, I certainly lucked out, because I could wash my hair and just let it dry naturally. These were the easiest hair years of my life — until cancer!

All this is to say: HAIR IS HIGHLY OVERRATED!

Back in the early part of the '90s my hair started going gray. At first I didn't mind because I still had a lot of natural curl, so the little bit of silver just added much needed highlights some women paid tons of money to acquire. Then I started getting sick — probably the beginning of fibromy-algia — and my hair lost a lot of its natural curl. What once had looked like highlights started to look like dingy streaks, making my face look drawn and thin.

That was when I thought maybe a little hair color would perk me up a bit. I started with a darker brown to match what had been my normal hair shade. Each time I bought color, I used a lighter shade until I was, bam bam, a blonde. I thought I looked terrific, but one day Trina and I watched the Vickie Lawrence Show, and I found out not everyone liked my look.

Vickie was changing everyone in the audience into different shades of red and auburn. It was a blast seeing all the remarkable makeovers. I looked at Trina and said, "How do you think I would look as a redhead?"

She rolled her eyes, "I think anything would be better than blonde."

Well, la-te-dah! Who died and made her queen? I wondered if she thought I was trying to compete with her. I decided to try out the red. At first it was neon, but then I settled on auburn, and for 14 years I used "Lightest Auburn" as MY color. It worked for me.

Then came cancer, chemo, and baldness.

When I learned I would be losing my hair, I didn't consider it would mean ALL hair: eyelashes and eyebrows, too. How come no one told me? That's the reason when you see cancer patients portrayed on television and in movies, they look like aliens: pale, wan, and lacking life. They don't have any hair on their entire faces. One day in January, I asked Ethan if he wanted a butterfly kiss. As I stretched to gently brush my lashes across his chubby little cheek, I thought, *Oh, my! I hope I have enough left to do the job.* I did, but not for long. Soon every small lash disappeared, and my eyebrows followed suit.

I mentioned before, it hurt to lose my hair. I don't mean emotionally. It literally hurt. My scalp tingled and stung even after I had my hair buzzed off. I had chosen for Cheryl to leave a stubble when she buzzed my hair, but I should have told her to remove all my hair completely. The most marvelous aspect of being bald, however, had to be showering. It turned out, for me anyway, there would be nothing quite like the warm shower spraying uninhibited over my slick, knob top. It was a heavenly feeling, and today I miss the lusciousness of the sweet sensation and actually envy all my bald male friends who get to experience that particular joy.

It didn't take long for me to grow accustomed to being bald. Around the house I wore baseball caps, and I purchased a wig soon after receiving the cancer diagnosis. It was a shorter version of my hair color and style. So many people told me they liked it better than my "real" hair I had to wonder just how bad I had looked before. About Christmas time I thought, *This is going to be a long period of wig-wearing. I think I want to have some fun with it.* So I asked Tom to take me to The Wig Shoppe again so I could select my present for under the tree . . . a wig that would give people pause: a blonde bob!

Before leaving with my purchase, Tom said, "Would you do me a favor? Would you just try on a silver gray wig?" I consented and was shocked when I loved the results. It had a tousled look. "This is probably what I would have looked like if I hadn't been playing around with brown, blonde, red, and auburn all those years." I didn't buy that wig then, but in February I returned and purchased what turned out to be my favorite hair.

It was fun to keep people guessing, "What is she going to look like today? Will she be Judy, her younger blonde sister, or Grams?" If I planned to meet someone, they would always ask before arriving at the final destination, "Who am I looking for today?"

I visited the store three different times, and each time it was packed with women, all either preparing to enter the cancer race or running for the finish line.

As my hair continued to diminish, I tried to replenish it by adding my own personal touch. I bought eyebrow pencils in blonde, auburn, and gray so my eye makeup would match whichever wig I was wearing. My eyelashes proved to be a little more difficult to reconstruct. I found some fake lashes at the drugstore; not wanting to look too much like a hussy, I chose the shortest and least thick so I would look halfway normal. When I first applied the little monsters, it took me the better part of a morning. I should have had lessons, but since I was doing it on my own, it was trial and error — a lot of both! About the time I'd get them glued and positioned correctly, my hand would tremble, causing one end to hike up and the other end to fall into my eye. With practice, I became adept at affixing the little boogers in the record time of 20 minutes! I was able to pull off the makeover most of the time, but occasionally I'd notice out of the corner of one eye, a shadow descending, and I would feel a slight obstruction with each blink. How embarrassing! Sure enough, when I would arrive home and look closely in the mirror, one side would have slid off, and be hanging precariously by a thin band of glue. I finally gave up on the lashes and only used them for fancy shindigs. I resorted to a good dose of eyeliner to make up for the lack of flutter power where my lashes should have been.

I thought I had mastered the art of "cover up" during the hairless days of treatment. Everywhere I went, people would act shocked when I told them I was in the midst of chemotherapy. "No, this isn't my real hair. It's a wig." I'd boast with some degree of pride. Pride that I had conquered the "chemo look."

Those who knew would bend over backward to compliment me, saying, "Judy, if I didn't know better, I'd think you were perfectly healthy. You look marvelous!" I couldn't hear that enough. After all, I worked tirelessly to look like I didn't have cancer, and I was pleased I had pulled it off.

However, there was also a side of me that struggled with the image I was portraying. I knew what I really looked like. It was all too obvious when I glanced in the mirror before I put on my wig, my eyebrows, my eyeliner, and the rest of the mask behind which I hid. Who was I kidding? Not me!

So, when my dearest friend, Yvonne Perry, came to visit me from New York toward the end of my chemotherapy treatments, I asked her one morning to take a "before and after" picture so I would have a permanent record of what it really was like to endure the bitterness of hair loss. She was the only one who mentioned a correction to my methodical makeover routine. "Judy, before I click the camera for the 'after' part, I need to tell you you're putting your eyebrows up way too high. They don't go there."

Really? How long had I been putting them "there" and looking like I was in a constant state of shock and surprise? Uh? Would anybody like to tell me?

I had truly missed Yvonne since she had moved from Louisville to be closer to her family. She had been my only source for honest evaluations, letting me know when I had snot hanging from my nose and flecks of food stuck between my teeth. It was natural for her to be the one to tell me my eyebrows were off kilter by a few degrees. But why did this revelation have to come so late in the game?

She took my pictures, and I got the graphic result I had wanted. They truly depicted the ravages of cancer and the flip side — the importance of looking "good" triumphing over desolation. I never tire of showing those shots and seeing the look of disbelief flood the faces of my friends. Ah-ha! I fooled them all!

CRAZY DAYS AND
CHEMO BRAIN

❀

I was ill prepared for much of the cancer journey. So much information was out there to digest, and I did not have enough energy to absorb what I needed to know. It seemed every day I was confronted with something out of the blue . . . surprise!

The doctor scheduled a second attempt to surgically insert the port for my chemo treatments. Because my low white-cell count had led to the cancellation of the first appointment, I made sure to have a blood test the day prior to the procedure. Everything looked like it was a go. I arrived at the hospital at 1:34 PM and was ready to be wheeled back to the operating room at 4:00. The IV lines were in my hand. I was wearing the teeny-tiny, open-in-the-back, cotton gown, and the nurse was waiting at the foot of my gurney. The doctor stood by my side going over last-minute details. Suddenly, a woman from the lab came rushing into the room yelling, "No! No! She can't go back." She held a piece of paper and shoved it under Dr. Hoagland's nose.

He looked at the report then at me. "Judy, I'm sorry. Your white count has bottomed out again, and I can't take a chance putting the port in right now. It would just be too dangerous."

The following Tuesday, I was scheduled for my second chemotherapy treatment, and I had to endure the poking and probing once again to find the perfect vein. I had only one left. During the second treatment, the administering nurse had to stay right by my side as she slowly pushed the "cocktail" through the syringe and into my body. It was a long procedure. The red solution, (which, if it seeps out onto the surrounding tissue, can burn and kill anything it touches), was treated as a bomb squad might treat a land mine. (An unexpected side effect was rosy pink urine for several days afterward.) Donna Gunnoe was right by my side, and I was so proud I had remembered when she arrived and when she left. I thought, *Maybe I'm getting the hang of this.*

Another friend, Donna Rosenberg, came to my rescue after the treatment, took me out for a bite to eat, and delivered me home to Shelbyville. When she left the house, I looked at my kitchen table and saw the mail and newspaper. *How did that get there?* I wondered. I vaguely remembered saying something about getting the mail as we pulled into the driveway, but as I wracked my brain over and over, I could not recall Donna taking care of this chore for me. I stared at the paper and uttered, "Well, at least I remember who was with me today during treatment, and I remember when they left. That's an accomplishment."

Since I had been having such a problem with low blood counts, my doctors decided I needed to have a boost to my system in the form of a Neulasta shot. So the next day, I drove into the hospital to get my first injection. They warned me the medicine could cause extreme joint and muscle pain. That didn't bother me. I'd suffered from the muscle pain of fibromyalgia for so many years it couldn't be that bad. Having had the second chemo treatment Tuesday, I started taking Kytril (for nausea) first thing Wednesday morning. The queasiness of the "second day after" was a little less than it had been Thanksgiving Day. Thursday evening, I reached up to my jaw line and found the glands below my ears were swollen and tender. Then I realized the tenderness radiated around behind my neck, down my spine, out my shoulders, and down my arms. I was miserable.

I got out the list of reasons to call the doctor and couldn't find anything resembling my situation. I called the hot-line number for the treatment center anyway, and they contacted my oncologist. He was at a loss to know what to tell me. He had never heard of this happening to anyone as a result of the chemo treatment or Neulasta. He advised me to keep checking my temperature through the evening and told me that if it spiked, I should go directly to the hospital.

Friday dawned, and I still had the swollen glands and tenderness, but I didn't feel as nauseous. I readied the house for my handy-dandy Dorothy who was scheduled to clean every other week. I made sure to keep the front door unlocked as I left with friends who came to pick me up for a visit to one of my favorite places, Irish Acres in Nonesuch, Kentucky.

It was a lovely day to make the 45-minute drive. I wore my auburn wig, and we dined on scrumptious food, browsing the antique mall after our leisurely meal. I nearly fainted as I walked down one of the hallways, so I left Donna Gunnoe and Shantha Diaz to shop without me as I sat at the front of the building sipping on a lemon-lime soft drink. My insides felt like an earthquake was rattling all my organs, and my head spun in circles. Later we stopped at a little store in Midway, and as I meandered through one of the quaint shops, I recognized the tell-tale signs of someone who had gone through chemo. She was the shop's owner, and she wore the cutest little cap with wisps of silver-white hair peeking out the sides. "Yep, chemo brain will get you every time," I heard her tell a customer. She went on to say she had finished her final treatment, and her hair was starting to grow back. Before her cancer, she had dark brown hair with only a few streaks of gray. Her new hair was coming in pure white. We discussed and compared medical notes then she asked, "Has the tiredness set in yet?" So that is what was wrong with me today!

We arrived back at my house, and I mentioned to the gals as we pulled into the driveway that my house would be clean. I got to the front door and started to put in the key but the door opened without needing to be unlocked. Dorothy had never forgotten to lock the door before! As I went into the house I could tell she had not been there to clean at all.

That had only happened one other time, and she had been

in the hospital with no way to tell me she couldn't make

it. Maybe something had happened to her again. I called

Dorothy's number, and her husband answered. I asked, "Is

Dorothy okay?" He assured me she was, so I asked that she

call me when she could. Dorothy called an hour later, and I

said, "Dorothy, I was just worried. I left the door unlocked

for you, but you never showed up."

She said, "Oh, I did show up, Judy. The door was locked.

I rang the doorbell and knocked and knocked, but no one

came, and I couldn't get in." I assured her it was unlocked.

She insisted it wasn't. I told Tom later I was concerned for

her mental health. Something was seriously wrong with her.

The door was not locked!

A few days later Dorothy came to the house to make-up

for her lost day. I was determined to get to the bottom of

the issue. As she stood in my kitchen I looked at her, and

it hit me like a bomb! I had left the door unlocked Friday.

Dorothy always came on Thursdays. I had a flashback to the

little shop in Midway and heard the shop owner say, "Yep,

chemo brain will get you every time." Chemo brain? Here

I had thought it was all Dorothy's fault. It was me! I apolo-

gized profusely. Fortunately for me, Dorothy had worked for

others who walked the chemo walk and she knew all about

the strange things it could do to the mind.

3700 — SOUND GOOD?

✹

After Christmas, Tom and I drove east to spend a week with our kids, the Sutherland family. We had a marvelous time in New Jersey, mostly chilling out with Maia and Gideon. Tom was able to get away for a few days to drive up to Connecticut where he took in a University of Connecticut (UCONN) girls' basketball game and visited friends and family.

I sat around and held Maia. I couldn't get enough of her. She had grown to 10 pounds, 4 ounces. Her coloring was good. The hole had closed slightly (.3 mm.), but we counted every little blessing. The doctors hadn't said anything more about open-chest surgery, but they had mentioned perhaps doing another valvuloplasty heart catherization.

We had been keeping tabs on a little girl who had been born four years earlier with the same problems as Maia. Her family had been members of our church in Louisville and had moved to Texas. It was good to know she was thriving and doing well after four years. However, she had to have an operation to update her shunts, so they would stretch with her growing body. Unfortunately, after the operation, a virus set in, and unable to fight the infection, she died.

Obviously, the news was very upsetting to us. Looking at Maia so rosy cheeked, lively and playful, we were soberly reminded her little heart was not perfectly whole yet. We began praying more earnestly that the Lord would touch her so she wouldn't have to endure further procedures. Nevertheless, we had to see the reality of her condition: the normal blood flow through a child's heart is in the 90s. Maia's was in the 20s and 30s. She had a way to go before we could breathe easily.

I was anxious to get back to Louisville so I could finally get the port installed for further chemo treatments. While in New Jersey, Gideon wanted to know why we had to leave so early. I told him I needed to have a hole put into my shoulder and a little tube inserted so all my "shots" could go into one hole and not be put in my arm and hand. He seemed to understand, but unfortunately Kenny didn't get in on that conversation. Later in the day, as they ran errands in the car, Gideon told Kenny, "Daddy, I don't think Gramma needs to go to 'Tucky to get her hole. She can get a hole here, don't you think? Dad? Dad?" Kenny was thinking, *What hole?*

We drove back home, and the next day I checked into the lab to have my blood work done. I entered the hallway with a smidgeon of fear and looking the technician in the eye, I said, "Okay, I need a good high number today."

He said, "Will 3700 do?" I couldn't believe it! I did a little Irish jig and a Pentecostal two-step right there in front of all the nurses. It was a happy day.

The next day the port went in without a hitch, and the day following I had my third chemo treatment. The oncologist met with me beforehand and mentioned I seemed to be handling everything well above normal. I wasn't sure what *normal* meant. If it meant I was keeping a positive attitude, I was doing my best. I had to attribute that to family and friends however. They kept me grounded in the Word and kept speaking wisdom and positive thoughts through e-mails and cards. Scriptures they called to my attention fed my soul. Their funny stories showered abundant laughter to my heart. Their needs reminded me to pray for others and to take my eyes off my own problems so I could focus on people with heartaches heavier than mine.

FLAPPING MY WINGS

※

I don't know what people did before computers and the ability to send out emergency calls for help over the Internet. After my third treatment, sometime about the third day — when the waves of pain and apprehension flooded my whole body, I went to the computer and sent out an SOS for prayer. I really wondered if I could survive the day without throwing in the towel.

The new motto I had created for myself, "I'd rather look good and feel bad than to feel good and look bad," didn't quite live up to my expectations at that moment. The Neulasta shot had certainly changed my mind concerning pain. It was a bad day, a very bad day. I wasn't feeling courageous or inspiring — something I had striven toward even in the worst circumstances. All I wanted to do was vegetate. I wrote, "Calgon, take me away!" Then I added, "Lord, I wait upon you so my strength will cause me to mount up with wings like the eagles. I will soar again . . . just not today." I returned to the fetal position in the recliner rocking chair, covered up with a throw, and waited for the end to come. Yes, it was that bad!

About an hour after spewing my troubles to all my friends and family, I struggled over to the computer to see if any words of wisdom were coming from the outer reaches of the Internet. I found at least 25 people had dropped what they were doing to pray, type out Scripture, give encouragement, tell me something funny, or share a story. I read each one and tears streamed down my face. What awesome friends! Some called me on the phone to say, "Judy, you can do this!" And they prayed. Oh, the power of prayer! I returned later in the evening to even more words of profound hope. Some typed out songs. One song I had forgotten has always been a favorite: "Turn your eyes upon Jesus, look full in His wonderful face, and the things of earth will grow strangely dim, in the light of His glory and grace." [3]

Another friend wrote about rising up on wings of eagles, and I was reminded of a song from long ago, written by friends: "It's time to fly. It's time to spread our wings and catch the wind of the spirit that's blowing through our lives." This was a test. I wasn't soaring, but I was trying desperately to flap my wings. I wanted to fly above the storm, not go through it.

My friends, Mel and Paulette Folkertsma, in California, sent these messages, "Okay, enough complaining! You could be with us, taking care of a strong-willed grand kid for a week. Then you would have something to complain about. Pray for us old codgers. We have learned the difference between a three year old and a terrorist . . . you can negotiate with a terrorist." Then they added, "Paul said something about this present distress lasting only a moment. He was speaking about the whole life. So you are enduring a millisecond — a nanosecond. Blink . . . it's gone!" The following day they wrote: "According to Paul, He (God) made us creatures subject to passions. All the pretense about being a super spiritual steady-Eddie is bunk in my opinion. I don't think Jesus was Mr. Steady. He got down. He got drained. He jumped for joy. He needed to get away from people once in a while. He looked for support at times. Don't think you have to be up all the time. Be what He created you to be, subject to passions. If you are down lower than you want to be, do just what you did and let the tribe of Judith know. Be honest. If past believers had not been down, I don't think we would have the book of Psalms. In a fallen world I think that is the way things are. We know you are going to make it."

Then Saturday arrived. Our church has three services: one Saturday evening and two Sunday morning. We usually went to the 9:00 Sunday morning service. By 8:00 Saturday evening, I started receiving calls and e-mails saying, "Judy, you have to go to church tomorrow morning because it is just for you!" Well, isn't that special? I hadn't planned on making it out the door.

Sunday morning, I slithered out of bed, and Tom and I made our way into Louisville. I told several "pew-mates" they could go home if they wanted because from what I had heard, the service was going to be just for me. I was very cynical about it all. Instead, from the first song ("Turn Your Eyes upon Jesus") to the last ("Turn Your Eyes upon Jesus"), I bawled like a baby. The poor people sitting behind me must have thought I had just lost my dearest friend. Every song, every Scripture, every prayer, and especially the sermon, were meant just for me. Selfish, isn't it, to think like that?

The theme for the service was "having courage in the midst of the storm." It was just perfect. The text was *Matthew 14:22*, "Jesus made the disciples get into the boat . . . ." He MADE them get in the boat. I had never noticed *made* before. Why would He have to force them to get into the boat? Evidently, they could see what was ahead — dark storm clouds rolling in. They were afraid even before they met the storm. They were afraid before they got into the boat. This little bit of insight amazed me.

One of the things about the "after burn" of chemo is you can't get rid of the nausea. When a woman goes through childbirth pains she has a precious little one to hold in her arms when it is over, and the bundle of joy instantly dims the memory of the agony she just suffered. All I had after four days of keel-over sick was the view ahead and the realization in another three weeks I would get to do it all over again. I knew what was to come. I could see those storm clouds gathering in the distance. It was not a pleasant thought, and it filled my heart with dread.

I mentioned my fear to our son Joel and he said, "Mom, by going through this you are persevering in order to hold your grandchildren in your arms." Later that evening, Joel slipped a CD into our sound system, and the most amazing music filled our house. He told us the symphony had been written by a friend, and she and her husband had taken it to a professional orchestra in Nashville to have it recorded. They had done all this for one person to hear. Can you imagine someone going to all that expense and exerting all that effort just for one person?

The music was a symphony of love. I cried through the whole CD. No words were sung — just heavenly, symphonic music depicting a man's life and his tragic story. The percussion resonated through the room. The strings lifted me up to the clouds. The woodwinds and brass swept over my soul like a harpist plucking tenderly at the strings of my life. It was as though God reached into my chest and wrung me out. I was literally transported out of the room into a place of holiness. *Ephesians 2:10* says, "For we are God's masterpiece. He has created us anew in Christ Jesus, so that we can do the good things he planned for us long ago (NLT)."

I was reminded of this Scripture as I listened to the ethereal music wafting through our home. In the margin of my Bible, I have written that the word for *masterpiece* in the original text means "poem or symphony." Beth Moore says about this verse, "Sooner or later it will all rhyme."

I'm not too sure my thinking God would orchestrate a weekend service just for me is too much out of the realm of possibility. In fact, when you think about it, He died just for me. He died just for you. Our former pastor's wife has a sign in her kitchen: "Fear not tomorrow for He is already there." He would be waiting for me at my next treatment, and I knew I could face the storm because He would be in the boat with me.

JUST THE FACTS

✵

My fourth chemotherapy session was scheduled in January. It turned out to be the day after Louisville experienced a few hours of ice followed by snow and even more ice. I wasn't sure the treatment center would be open, but I was encouraged to come in if I could get there because more snow and ice were in the forecast later in the evening. The doctors were concerned the office wouldn't be open the next day. Rather than have the treatment in the morning, however, they moved me back to the afternoon. Because of the revised schedule, I had Tom drop me off at the hospital so I could visit with Donna Gunnoe's husband,

Don, who was recovering from emergency five-bypass heart surgery.

After my visit, I walked through the hospital and entered the pedway connecting the hospital with the treatment center. Entering the waiting room was eerie. Usually it was packed with patients, but that day there were only five. A skeleton crew was on duty, and it was much too quiet. The routine was to have blood work, see the doctor, and then go to the treatment room for the chemotherapy. I decided since there were fewer patients, I'd venture asking the doctor some questions that had been weighing on my mind. He was more than accommodating, answering everything I asked in a slow, deliberate manner.

Many people had been asking me questions I could not answer, so I decided I needed to educate myself to be able to respond appropriately to interrogators. I found out the type of cancer I had was estrogen based. In fact, my estrogen levels scored a very high 97 percent. More sobering, though, was finding out estrogen-based cancer can return, which was why they were treating me so aggressively. The doctor explained I would be taking Arimidex the rest of my life. For me, Arimidex would be more effective than Tamoxifen, the common follow-up medication. I would be put on a decreasing schedule of check-ups for the following five years. As we talked, the doctor asked me if I knew the difference between Stage III and Stage IV cancer. I told him I assumed Stage IV meant the cancer had reached the lymph nodes and had spread to other areas of the body. He said, "Actually, there is a simpler way of putting it. Stage III is curable. Stage IV is not." He continued, "That doesn't mean Stage IV patients can't live a long, productive life, but they need continuous scans and a higher form of long-term maintenance."

I begged and pleaded (nearly cried), trying to convince him to not give me the Neulasta shot. But it was to no avail. He did say because I'd had such nausea, he would prescribe a new medication, Emend, which he felt would combat the upset stomach. I didn't start my chemo treatment until 2:00 PM and when the nurse inserted the needle to establish a pure blood line in my new port, only old blood returned. So she tried flushing the line with saline only to have me grab my chest and groan with pain. It scared her and the other nurses enough that they stopped the flushing altogether and called in the doctor for a conference. It was decided to dispense with the port and give the chemo through a vein in my hand — again. I knew finding a vein would be a problem since so many had blown out on previous attempts. The first one they used blew immediately. They tried a vein close to the knuckle of my index finger. It blew, too. They finally had to call on an expert to find a vein and hook me up. Tom arrived around 5:30 in the late afternoon to take me home.

The ice began falling that night, and at 8:00 the next morning our electricity went off. We hunkered down with blankets and sat by the fireplace reading books. My friend

Debbie Kaupp works for Jerry Jenkins in Colorado Springs, and she had sent me his latest book, *Riven*. It was perfect timing for delving into an intriguing plot line. Regardless of the suspense of the novel, by early evening, when I couldn't feel my nose any longer, we gathered some things together and drove down the road to spend the night with Reta and Norm Stivers who lived in one of the patio homes I had sold.

Nearly a million people in the Louisville area were without power for several days. We only endured one night of discomfort. What a blessing! A week later thousands still suffered in extreme cold. More than 25 people lost their lives from mistakes in the use of alternative power sources (generators and charcoal grills) and being careless with candles. The countryside resembled a region a tornado had hit. The woods behind our house looked like a winter wonderland from the sun's rays hitting the icy branches, but we heard sounds like gun shots as the trees split and those crystal-covered branches fell.

I came out of the Neulasta stupor much quicker after the fourth treatment, and the staff at the treatment center told me the worst was behind me. The last four treatments would be of a different "cocktail," and the symptoms shouldn't be so severe. I was so glad to hear the news, I decided right then and there, if they were lying to me, it would be "off with their heads!"

OFF WITH THEIR HEADS!

✸

B efore my fifth treatment, I developed a cough and chest congestion that postponed the repair of my port and caused the oncologist to delay my chemotherapy. Each day, instead of getting better, I got worse. Finally, I called the nurses at the treatment center, and they thought it would be best to schedule me for a chest X-ray. The X-ray did not show any signs of pneumonia, but when the oncologist listened to my lungs, he said, "Oh boy, there are a lot of 'Rice Krispies' going on in there." (Meaning he could hear the "snap, crackle and pop" of congestion.) He also witnessed the tremendous cough that had kept me up most nights and resulted in pulled back muscles and a burst eardrum.

The cough had been very debilitating. I tried to sleep on an incline, so I could achieve better air flow. However, the previous night I had awakened every 30 minutes, not from coughing, but from the sensation of being strangled. I would have to purposefully cough to rearrange the mucous, clearing my windpipe for easier breathing. I would fall back to sleep only to be awakened again and again. I could tell the doctor was frustrated and quite adamant that I couldn't go through with the chemo treatment. He fumbled around with his thoughts about what he might prescribe to help break up the congestion. He finally settled on Z Pak.

The doctor told me if I showed even slight improvement by Friday of that week, they would try to go ahead with the chemo treatment. Consequently, my entire schedule would have to be adjusted, changing my regular treatment day from Tuesday to Friday, which would be much handier for Tom. Friday was his day off, and he would be able to accompany me to all future treatments, so I would no longer have to call on my friends for transportation. I was looking forward to having him experience what I dealt with every three weeks. It also meant surgery to fix my port would be postponed until I could get my white-blood count up again. I was having more and more difficulty remembering what *normal* felt like. It shouldn't have surprised me I got sick since my resistance to infections was laid perilously low by having my white-blood count annihilated on a routine basis. The cough was so bad I feared my fifth treatment would be canceled again.

Tom and I arrived at 8:15 Friday morning, and I started having the "Rice Krispies" rattling throughout my chest. The nurse listened and didn't seem too concerned, giving me the "all clear" to go into the treatment room. She did say I would not be having the Neulasta shot, and at the news I was nearly out of my mind with happiness. Donna Gunnoe had reminded me earlier in the week that during the orientation they had mentioned I would graduate from the treatment chair to a bed for the last four sessions. As I walked into the vast room of patients, the nurse directed me to select a bed over against a bank of windows. This was an indication I was about to embark on a whole new routine. I sank down into the mattress, struggling to get comfortable.

They started the chemo preparation by 10:30 AM, and I wasn't finished until 2:30 in the afternoon, making it a six-hour procedure. We had rushed out of the house without eating breakfast thinking I would be through with my treatment before lunch. Even with the treatment center's refrigerator packed with snacks, I couldn't bring myself to munch on anything. Tom was satisfied with an apple, soft drinks, and juice. The premeds took as long to administer as the entire treatments I received the first four sessions. They doped me up good before flushing the line, and started me on the new cocktail. That took two hours, and another flushing followed .

They hooked me up to a blood pressure monitor, and as the new solution dripped into my veins, my blood pressure started sailing higher and higher. Each time it went up, I started coughing. I was embarrassed. There I was, surrounded by sick people on either side, and my cough sounded just like it had earlier in the week. I couldn't suppress it at all. I tried desperately to confine the mist escaping my mouth with each hack by burying my head in the blankets and pillow.

Changing my appointments from Tuesdays to Fridays was a big disappointment for me as I had gotten into a comfort zone. I asked the Lord to show me why this bump in the road had to take place. This day He made it abundantly clear. My friend, Susie Dana, had told me she shied away from the breast-cancer support groups because they tended to turn into pity parties. She said she received more encouragement from those who were receiving treatment during chemo days. Although I had been looking for the same camaraderie at my Tuesday appointments, each time I saw different people, and most of them preferred reading and sleeping over conversation. When I settled down for the Friday treatment, I noticed a lovely young woman in the bed to my right. The curtain was partially pulled for privacy, so I didn't get to introduce myself. Soon, however, as she walked with her IV pole to the bathroom, she stopped at the foot of my bed and asked, "Do y'all go to Southeast Christian Church?" Tom was wearing his Master's Men Southeast Christian Church sweatshirt that had already been the source of talk in the waiting room. (He had been a member of the 100-voice choir for 15 years.) It didn't hurt having Tom with me anyway as he is known to never meet a stranger and starts conversations with everyone he meets.

I replied to this lovely gal standing at the foot of my bed, "Yes, we attend Southeast Christian." She mentioned the church's Easter pageant and introduced herself as Lisa* and her husband, Jake* who was with her. They traveled from a small town in Indiana every three weeks for her chemotherapy. As we talked, I learned both Lisa and I were taking our fifth treatment. Since we were going to be on the same schedule, we promised to save beds next to each other for future sessions. We pulled back the curtain permanently and between each of us dozing off, we talked, and Tom and Jake never ran out of things to discuss.

As we visited, I found out Lisa was only 41 years old. She and Jake had two daughters, one to be married to their pastor's son in June. Her goal was to grow her hair back in time for the wedding. The previous summer she started having problems with her digestion and lost 30 pounds in two months. Her doctors started running tests, mainly to her stomach and kidneys, thinking the problem had to be there. She had over 100 biopsies to her stomach alone. Finally a doctor got the idea they needed to check outside her stomach, and they found cancer wrapped around several ducts. It was not the primary source, however, and one doctor remembered on a previous mammogram a ridge had shown up. Thinking it wasn't anything of consequence, the doctor had let it pass without further research. Lisa had a biopsy of the breast area and the source was discovered. They also found the cancer had spread to her uterus and lymph nodes. Her cancer was Stage IV.

Lisa's attitude was amazing, and she displayed a contagious love for Jesus and an abiding faith. We talked of spiritual matters until I was dismissed for the day, but before leaving we gathered around Lisa's bed for a time of prayer. Now I know the Lord had all this in mind from the beginning, and I wasn't at all upset my schedule had been changed. It was wonderful to meet other patients who were eager to talk and share experiences with us, and it was downright great to have Tom with me since the new process was more tiring than I had anticipated. I needed his strength and his humor to get me through the day.

The first two days after the fifth treatment I was shaky, weak, and nauseated, but it wasn't bad. I started to think they had been right about the side effects being lighter than the first four treatments. Unfortunately, Sunday evening I began to have sharp pains in my toes and feet. The pain progressed into my ankles and then both knees. As the evening wore on, the pain became agony and settled into my back, hips, shoulders, and even my hands and fingers. Tom prayed for me twice. It was the most restless, sleepless night I'd had.

I called the doctor first thing Monday morning, and they gave the nod to take as much pain medication as I felt I needed. The narcotics helped, but the discomfort was to the level even my teeth hurt. The doctor said he believed the new chemo solution had stirred up a storm within my system that brought out the fibromyalgia full force. I sent out an e-mail plea to all my family and friends to be praying I could get through the days ahead. If I could forecast how long the pain would last, I could deal with it. Unfortunately, I didn't know how long I would have to endure. That had always been a stumbling block for me: if I knew how long I had to suffer, I could endure for the sake of the prize. As far as I was concerned, it was OFF WITH THEIR HEADS!

AND BABY MAKES FIVE
❀

I finally came out of the fog enough to make plans for the following Friday. I would get my blood work done at the treatment center then we would drive into the heart of Louisville and visit with baby Kaya, who was still in the NICU at the teaching hospital in downtown Louisville. We made arrangements to meet Joel, Toby, and their little boy, Ethan, at the hospital, and then go out to eat as a family. We were all excited because it was Toby's last day teaching fourth grade before her maternity leave. Joel called us right before we left the clinic. "Mom, I just found out Toby called her parents to pick her up from her school because she's having contractions, and she was afraid to drive her car home. We are going to have to take a rain check on our evening together."

I told him that was fine and to just keep us informed on her progress. I thought it would take a while for her to deliver this baby because she was in labor with Ethan for many hours. We would just go on downtown, see Kaya, grab a bite to eat, and then go on to a hospital in the suburbs for the happy arrival. Fifteen minutes later my cell phone rang. It was Joel, "Mom, Toby's mom just called, and they have Toby in the car. Her contractions are 30 seconds apart, so they aren't going to take her home. They're taking her straight to the hospital."

"Good idea," I counseled.

We went on into downtown Louisville for our visit with Micah, Gina, and Kaya. Because I'd been so sick with the respiratory infection, I hadn't had a chance to see Kaya for several weeks. We were surprised at how much she had grown. It was March 6, and she had been in the NICU since

January 21. We were pleased to hear the talk around the unit

was that within two weeks she would be allowed to go home.

I was holding and rocking Kaya when my phone rang again.

Again it was Joel telling me they had arrived at an east-end

hospital, and instead of setting Toby up in a labor room, she

was being taken directly to delivery. Tom and I hustled out,

as did Micah and Gina. We weren't in the waiting room more

than five minutes before Joel came out with his arms spread

wide saying, "Only four pushes! Four!"

Benjamin Thomas weighed 7 pounds, 14 ounces and was

21 inches long. Although the kids had mentioned earlier that

they were going to name the baby *Benjamin*, Tom hadn't

been told prior to this that they intended to use *Thomas* as

his middle name, so he was quite pleased. Then Tom sur-

prised them with the news that *Benjamin* was Tom's grand-

father's name. They had no idea that both names were part of

Gerdis family history. What a blessing! When my adventure

through cancer began I was the grandmother of two. Within

five months, I had become the grandmother of five!

FLUSHED

❀

Saturday after the big birthday, I woke up to redness in my left hand. As the day wore on, the crimson deepened and streaks of pink extended to my fingers. I watched it closely, and Monday I called the treatment center and spoke with a nurse. She quizzed me about everything that had transpired since my chemo treatment and subsequent blood work, which had been drawn a week later. It was like playing a detective game — piecing together all the clues and trying to come up with a solution.

Near the end of my last chemo treatment, my male nurse, Mark,* had come to my bedside to tell me he would be leaving for lunch and while he was gone another nurse would check my IVs. When the bag was empty, she would then flush out my lines (a 30-minute procedure) before sending me home. Everyone nearby remembered his explanation because he wasn't sure he would be back by the time I was dismissed. When my IV bag emptied, a nurse came over, and rather than starting the flush, she began to disconnect all the lines. I told her I needed to be flushed first. She told me I had already been flushed out. I told her I hadn't, and Mark had made it very clear I needed a flush before I left. She looked at my records and pronounced me flushed, saying there was no need to do it again.

What was I to do? Defy her authority? Ask for another nurse? Ask for a doctor? Hindsight indicated I should have done all three. Overhearing my conversation with the second nurse, my new chemo mate, Lisa, was very upset. I gathered all my things and asked her to tell Mark when he returned to the treatment room, that I didn't get flushed. When the elevator opened, Mark stepped off. I stopped him and told him I suspected I had not had my lines flushed out. He said he would check with the nurse when he got to the treatment room. He requested neither that I accompany him nor that I stay in the hall until he could resolve the dilemma. I went on home and thought nothing more about the experience.

A week later, I checked in for my regular blood work. Instead of the normal prick to my finger I was told by the technician she needed to draw blood from the top of my hand because she had to retrieve several vials. The next day, I awoke to the redness in my hand and streaks leading to my fingers. It resembled a severe burn. When the nurse solved the puzzle, she asked me to come directly to see her. She felt by not having had the flush, the Taxatier had remained in my veins and caused the inflammation.

I received a red-carpet welcome. Even my oncologist came out to give his opinion. Pictures were taken of my hand. They upped the dosage of antibiotics and required me to go back three days in a row for shots to boost my immune system. I was instructed to watch my hand closely, and if I noticed the redness progressing up my arm, I was to call immediately and report to the hospital emergency room. The main concern was that I would develop cellulitis, a serious bacterial skin infection that can spread into the bloodstream and become life threatening if left untreated. Another problem? The previously scheduled repositioning of my port had to be canceled for the third time. The port that would have prevented all this from happening in the first place had it been functioning properly from the beginning.

GONE WITH THE WIND
❀

B enjamin was born a week after my fifth chemo treatment. Because of our busy schedule that evening, Tom and I hadn't had a chance to grab a bite to eat, so hoping Benjamin would hold off for a few minutes before entering this world, we stopped at a restaurant across the street from the hospital. We chose a restaurant that features breakfast anytime of the day, so my mouth was watering for a nice meal of scrambled eggs, link sausage, and country biscuits.

The server brought our food, and I took a bite of the eggs first. I gagged. What in the world? Something was seriously wrong. I took a bite of the sausage. Again, the most horrid taste exploded in my mouth. What could be more benign than a biscuit? I ventured a mouthful and spit it out. I thought there was something wrong with the food, so I asked Tom to take a bite. He disagreed with my assessment, pronouncing the meal delicious. That could mean only one thing — my taste buds had vanished. Friends had told me at some point I could develop a metallic taste while eating, but this was not just a tinge of metal. This was full blown bitterness at its worst. I tried valiantly to get something down. Nothing I did made the vittles taste remotely edible. Our server came to refill my water glass and asked if something was wrong. I felt like bawling but held my tears, "I'm so sorry. But I'm having difficulty with my taste buds. I've had chemotherapy in the last week, and I guess I'm experiencing the side effects of my last treatment. I can't eat this. I'm sure nothing is wrong with it, but I can't look at it either. Would you please take it away?" I wanted to put my head on the table, but I knew better. The server returned later with a chocolate ice-cream sundae. I was able to get a portion down before we left for the hospital waiting room.

There are few things in my life I like more than eating. I love to try new foods and recipes. Other than breaded stewed tomatoes, most anything would rank as a favorite. The days following the decline of my ability to taste food, I sampled dozens of delicacies, trying to decide if I could abide the metallic sensation each item elicited. When I had experienced nausea, I was still able to taste and receive nourishment. This, however, was a whole new problem. I needed nourishment, so I forced myself to eat purely from necessity. Eventually, I found one item I could eat with a semblance of enjoyment. That was the mango smoothie from Panera Bread. Anything excessively sweet turned to tin in my mouth, so I avoided food with even a hint of sugar. I lost 42 pounds before my ability to taste food returned.

One day I prepared a lovely meal of sirloin steak, baked potatoes, and garden vegetables. I couldn't swallow the baked potato because the natural starches turned to sour mush in my mouth. And the steak? It was good thing I had learned to cope with liver every once in a while, because the steak bordered on the chalky texture of that oft maligned delicacy.

Another evening we took Micah out to eat at a local barbeque restaurant. With the first bite, I had to lay aside the fork. What sorrow for this southern girl to realize she couldn't bring one morsel to her lips. The saddest day occurred when late one evening I was drawn to Girl Scout Thin Mint Cookies. I swear I heard them calling from my kitchen pantry. Nothing tastes so good to this former Girl Scout than those chocolate coated wafer thins. It was late. I had been reading in bed. I tiptoed because I knew if Tom heard me, he would be right there to get his share. Opening the brand new package of cellophane-wrapped treats, I thought, *Just two. That's all I need.* I cradled the pair gently in the palm of my hand as I traipsed back to the bedroom. I propped myself up with pillows and prepared to bite into the first round. What did I experience? The biggest disappointment! I tasted nothing more than the flavor of a communion wafer. That was it! It didn't taste bad; it had no taste, just nothing. Then I cried.

PORT OF CALL

❀

Finally, port day arrived. Three times the repositioning had been delayed. It was finally going to happen, and I was pleased as punch. I was in the preop cubbyhole — flat on my back. One of the nurses came in, and I glanced up at her. She looked familiar, but I was looking at her upside down. Where had I seen her before? Ahhh . . ., "I know you! You are the 'poop' nurse!"

She looked at me and gasped, "Oh, my goodness. I can't believe it's you. I've got something to give you. Stay right here. Don't go anywhere." Where did she think I was going?

She returned a few seconds later with a gift card to the hospital coffee shop. "I had this made up for you because of what happened. I didn't think I'd ever see you again. What are you doing here?"

I explained I was there to have my port repositioned because it wasn't working. Her name was Peggy, and she started getting me ready to go back to the operating room. It took over an hour for five nurses and one doctor to get an IV line running. At first Peggy tried. She stuck my left arm three times. She went for the underside of my wrist and then twice up at the elbow. When she was unsuccessful, she called for help. A gal named Brenda came in and three other nurses who were nearby and idle at the time, decided to give Peggy support and console me with hand holding and encouragement.

Brenda's first attempt was a disaster. She tried somewhere between my wrist and the bend in my elbow. She thought she had it and began the fluid drip only to have me writhing in pain. A huge knot swelled up on my arm, so they pulled out the needle. Everyone was apologizing. She tried two more times on the underside of my arm, once toward the outside, and the last time way over to the outside of my elbow. It was agonizingly painful. In the middle of all this, I asked them to please call Tom out in the waiting room to tell him to pray and to call our prayer team at church. They did and he did.

They kept saying, "Girl, do you ever need a working port!" No joke! When they had exhausted all their options, they called the anesthesiologist from the operating room. She looked at my bruised, bleeding, swollen left arm and quickly decided there would be no more poking and probing. The only remaining site would be the right side of my neck. I cringed, "Will this hurt?"

"Yes," they all said in unison.

It did. I came so close to crying, but, I didn't. Once it was in, I felt no pain. Of course, they started filling me up with the most luscious relaxing meds they had available to try to make amends. During the surgery, Dr. Hoagland realized the port he had implanted earlier was a dud, and he had to

replace it with a new one. I was just glad to get it done. Was

that a break in the storm clouds above my head? I think I saw

a small ray of sunshine.

THE MIDNIGHT HOUR

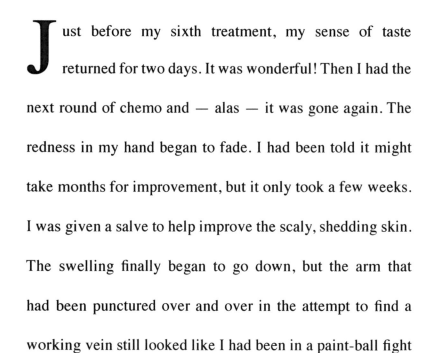

J ust before my sixth treatment, my sense of taste returned for two days. It was wonderful! Then I had the next round of chemo and — alas — it was gone again. The redness in my hand began to fade. I had been told it might take months for improvement, but it only took a few weeks. I was given a salve to help improve the scaly, shedding skin. The swelling finally began to go down, but the arm that had been punctured over and over in the attempt to find a working vein still looked like I had been in a paint-ball fight and lost. The good news was the port worked like a charm for my treatment. If it hadn't, I don't know what they would have done about administering the chemotherapy, because I had no more options to insert an IV.

My white blood count dropped so dramatically after my fifth treatment, I was told I had to have another Neulasta shot, which was troubling since it had caused so much discomfort the previous time. I recalled I had just wanted someone — anyone — to hit me over the head, knock me out, and end my misery. To help counter the pain, the doctor put me on a steroid pack. I asked him what the side effects would be. He thought for a second, "Ummm. Let's see . . ., restless sleep, edginess, tenseness, agitation, feeling . . . um . . . cranky." What he didn't tell me was included on the information attached to the prescription: "bloating, weight gain, swelling of face and hands," and the list continued. It appeared to me the treatment might be worse than the original pain.

That day, my chemo partner, Lisa, and her husband, Jake, had been at the center since 7:30 AM, so by the time I got back to the treatment room they were already settled in a private alcove just around the corner from my bed. Even though we weren't side by side, we took advantage of every potty break to visit, and Tom and Jake went off together for lunch. Lisa had the cutest wig, but bless her heart, she made the mistake of opening a hot oven door to extract a casserole and forgot to remove her wig first. The heat had singed off her bangs. For that reason, I always tried to remember to wear my baseball caps around the house. I couldn't be too careful with those wigs, especially around high heat. They could melt into a synthetic wad if exposed to high temperatures.

As I waited to see if the steroid pack and the pain pills would alleviate my suffering after the sixth treatment, I counted down the hours and then the minutes. By Sunday evening, I began to think I had dodged the bullet. I had a few twitches of discomfort here and there but nothing serious. I went to bed around 11:00, but by midnight I knew it was coming on strong — *pain*, that is — searing, penetrating pain.

Have you ever tried to sleep with pain radiating from your feet up to your jaw? It isn't easy. I took the prescribed pain pills and started levitating above the bed. That's when the Lord came. I didn't sing out loud — just in my spirit, "Blessed assurance, Jesus is mine,! O, what a foretaste of glory divine!" (my favorite hymn). I didn't sing it like they do when a music director feels the need to keep the tempo moving. I sang with great feeling and emotion, swelling above my bed from deep within my soul. "Okay, that was good, but I've got to come up with another song." I muttered to myself.

I don't know why, but a song from 40 years in my past percolated and bubbled over in my mind: "Once in the stillness of the late midnight hour, I felt the presence of the Lord's saving power; I fell on my knees, and cried to Him there, Oh, merciful Savior, hear a low sinner's prayer. Well, every hour and every day, well every moment, in every way;

I'm leaning on Jesus the rock of my soul, I'm singing His

praises wherever I go."[4] I tried and tried to think . . . why did

I come up with *that* song?

Back in what now seems like the dark ages, I lived in Hot

Springs, Arkansas, where my family would drive to Little

Rock for "all-night singings." I was a teen the first time I

attended one of those gospel concerts, and I thought we liter-

ally would be up all night. How exciting was that? I learned

"all night" meant until midnight or no later than 1:00 in the

morning. Regardless of the hour, it was a great thrill to hear

my favorite singers like The Imperials, The Stamps Quartet,

The Blackwoods, and many others. I don't remember which,

but one of those groups sang "Every Hour and Every Day."

Some time later, a trio I sang with at Hillcrest Children's

Home (where my dad was the administrator) adopted the

song and sang it at church, at our chapel services, and when

we went on tour with the Home's choir. For decades, that

song had lain dormant in my memory, and it resurfaced just when I needed it.

My theme song for my cancer journey became "You Never Let Go." Our church had started singing it before I was diagnosed with cancer. I had no idea how important it would become in my faith walk. When we sang it during my cancer treatments, my heart would melt, and it would be just me and Jesus. It was the last song I sang after midnight on Friday. It took me into sweet slumber.

What I found comforting in that song was I didn't have to hold on. He was holding on to me, and He would never let go. He didn't let me go that night, or the next day and night, or the day after. The pain continued for more than 48 hours, but it was so much more bearable. I endured. He came to me after midnight, held on to me, and carried me through the torrential rain. The next day I opened my e-mail to see a message from a dear friend in Brussels who is a quadriplegic. Her message brought tears to my eyes:

"I am reminded of *Psalm 42:8*. 'By day the Lord directs his love, at night his song is with me – a prayer to the God of my life.' When I am unable to sleep, His song is there. May you have eyes to see His loving kindness towards you and the ability to recognize and pull up the song that is hidden in *your* heart."

THIS, TOO, SHALL PASS

W ith each chemotherapy treatment my difficulty eating became more pronounced. It was with great effort I would choke down a muffin with a little raspberry jam for breakfast, a bite or two of leftovers for lunch, and a few bites of dinner.

One Thursday morning, I began the usual routine, toasting a muffin, brewing some coffee, and settling down at the table with the newspaper. With my first bite, I knew something was seriously wrong. I had to toss the muffin because I felt like I was eating sandpaper. I had some fruit and yogurt in the refrigerator, so I tried whipping up a smoothie. I could take only two sips before gagging. Tom had had a late meeting to attend in Louisville. He called while driving home, and I told him I was in a world of trouble finding anything I could eat. Reluctantly, I asked him to return to Panera in town to purchase a mango smoothie. He was such a sweetheart to get off at the next exit and retrace his steps just to bring his wife something I could eat.

At bedtime I noticed that merely swallowing hurt my throat tremendously. I felt almost like I had an abscess or a painful growth in my throat. I was thoroughly perplexed at what could be causing me so much discomfort. I knew I had an appointment at the treatment center for 2:30 Friday afternoon, so I didn't try to eat anything all day. When I arrived for my blood work, I told the receptionist I needed to see someone about my mouth and throat. After my blood was drawn, I went straight to the treatment room and signed in. My favorite nurse, Missy, was assigned to check me out. As I started describing my problem, she reached for a flashlight and asked me to open my mouth. When I complied, she

jumped back, "Yup, just what I thought! You have thrush."

"Thrush? I thought only babies got that!"

She came back a few minutes later and handed me a pre-

scription for Nystatin. When I saw the name printed out, I

cringed. Nearly 20 years prior I had been on Nystatin, and it

had been a gruesome experience, ingesting the bitter powder

mixed with water several times a day. I shuddered remem-

bering the awful concoction.

Before I left, I remembered why I had come into the

clinic in the first place: to have my blood work done. I called

out, "Missy, what about my blood results?"

She hurriedly ran over to the computer to print off the

sheet showing all my stats. She carried it as she approached

me, saying, "You aren't going anywhere for a little while."

I looked at the figures, paying special attention to the

WBC (white blood count). It read 3.85L. That meant my

count was at 3,850. That was good! Missy pointed to the "L"

immediately after the count. I had never seen the *L* before.

She explained normally it would be a good count, but the L

meant another figure count rendered the WBC number nil. I

looked further down the page, and there it was, a big fat *zero*.

Missy had me sit down while she went off to find a

doctor. It didn't take long for him to come out and explain

they would be putting me on a powerful antibiotic, and I was

told I would need to stay away from people — especially

sick people — until my count went back up.

Interestingly, both Kaya and Benjamin had thrush, and

the following evening Kaya came to visit "Zsa Zsa" (the

name Ethan had given me as he learned to talk). Setting

on the kitchen counter was my big bottle of Nystatin; next

to it was a little dropper bottle of Nystatin for Kaya. Both

vials were filled with a citrus-flavored solution, not the bitter

powder I remembered from by-gone days. Regardless, you

couldn't have proved it by me because I could taste nothing.

I tortured myself most evenings by watching Rachael Ray of "Rachael's Vacation" or Guy Fieri of "Diners, Drive-ins and Dives" as they ate wonderful food in far-away, exotic places. Then I would fall asleep and dream of scrumptious, mouth-watering vittles all night long. It didn't matter how much I ate in my slumber, I lost weight. And so did Maia. Trina had called, asking us to pray she would start gaining. The growth of her tiny little frame had come to a standstill. Heart babies can have a difficult time gaining because their little hearts are working so hard to function. They began making plans to put Maia on a caloric supplement. I thought it might be a good idea for me to do the same.

When I sent out my regular "newsletter" titled "This Too Shall Pass," I heard from our friends in California, Mel and Paulette Folkertsma: " 'This, too, shall pass' is only for those with kidney stones."

Smarty pants!

EMBRACING PAIN

✵

When I was told I would probably experience numbness in my extremities with the new treatment, I thought: *That's better than having pain.* Then, I remembered a lesson in pain the Lord had taught me several years earlier when my aunt contracted leprosy. Yes, she had *leprosy*. We were all shocked when my cousin, Anne, called one Christmas day to tell us my Aunt Ruth's diagnosis. She had been in the hospital for a long time undergoing tests; finally, they had an answer. No one knows how she happened to succumb to this horrible disease, but as we soon learned, it can lie dormant for as long as 10 years before symptoms of the disease appear. A leprosy colony is located in Louisiana, but my aunt was allowed to stay in the hospital in St. Louis after the administration requested to keep her. No one on their staff had ever seen the disease, since it was a teaching hospital, she became a prime exhibit.

I started doing research on leprosy and found out much of what I thought I knew was false. When I thought of the lepers in the Bible, I thought about their being highly contagious, having open sores, losing limbs, and being outcast from society. What I discovered in my reading was leprosy actually attacks the nerves of the body, going to the extremities first. A lot of pain is associated with the disease, but once those nerves die, numbness settles in. Leprosy does not involve sores, open wounds, or loss of limbs. Actually, they are side effects caused by the numbness. In Third-World countries where leprosy is more common, those who have reached the numbness state are unaware, for instance, that they've stepped on a nail or a piece of glass, tearing open the skin on the bottoms of their feet. They might drop something into a fire and, without thinking, just reach in and take it out. One person was known to be trying to open a gate and rammed a nail into the palm of his hand. Because those afflicted with leprosy do not feel pain, they fail to get treatment, thus infection sets in, and eventually they lose their fingers, toes, hands, or feet.

Through my study of leprosy, I'd learned pain is a gift, and I must try to embrace it. Notice, I said, *try*. It can be difficult to run to, rather than away from, pain. I knew My heavenly Father had planned for my greater good through all this. Donna Gunnoe sent me a prayer I've taken as my own. It goes like this:

"Father, I confess that I don't like suffering, pain, disappointment, persecution or sorrow. I do, however, believe that your promises are true. I hold on to the promise that the glory you have in store for me is far greater than the difficulties I face. Strengthen me for the days ahead and use me to bring you glory no matter what my current situation may be. In Jesus' name I pray. Amen."

After all, I was created for the sole purpose of glorifying Him. That's it. The end of the story. No need to go any further. If I couldn't glorify Him in all situations, I couldn't fulfill my purpose. I'm so glad I found Him (or He found me), and He is walking along the path with me. Knowing He was there made the difficult times so much easier, and knowing that the stripes He bore on His back were for my healing, brought a surge of faith to my weary heart.

JOY COMES IN
THE MORNING

I started noticing unusual pain to the knuckles on my right hand one evening as I prepared for bed. Just the mere act of pulling the sheets up caused a burning sensation that radiated from my finger tips to my wrist. My knuckles were bright red as though I had scalded them in boiling water. In the morning, the redness had advanced down the side of my hand toward my wrist and from my thumb down my arm. Then I started having problems with my toes. I couldn't bear to have anything touch my feet. Within two days, I experienced the same sensations in my left hand. Sensitivity set into the tips of my fingers. If I had an ear itch and tried to use my finger to scratch, I would pull back in pain. My fingers were so painful I couldn't push the buttons on my touch-tone phone.

Think about all you do with your finger tips. I never knew how essential that little area of the body is to daily activities. Among those activities are applying make-up, scratching an itch, buttoning and unbuttoning a garment, playing the piano, typing, opening a snap-on lid, opening the drier. The list is endless.

I went into the treatment center, and after a three-hour wait a nurse saw me. She was immediately concerned with my red, blistered hands because of my previous blood work. She called for a doctor. They checked my blood again. My count was up and normal. The doctor believed that since I'd had this type of burn before it was a reaction to the Taxatier. They said they had never seen anyone with this reaction before. Therefore, he thought I shouldn't continue with the prescribed treatment. He would be talking to the other doctors about changing my treatment to another "cocktail." I learned finger-tip sensitivity is a common side effect of Taxatier, which has a tendency to create havoc with all the extremities. The nurse asked me if I had noticed any puss coming from under my nails. I told her I hadn't and asked why?

She said, "Oh, sometimes Taxatier will cause the nails to buckle and fall off."

I was horrified! I had been a nail biter for 50 years, but for the past 13 years, I'd stopped biting and had prided myself in sporting pretty manicured nails. I refused to believe my nails would suffer such a terrible demise. Losing my hair? I was okay with that, but losing my nails, I decided, was not going to happen.

My seventh treatment day rolled around, and my "cocktail" was changed to Taxol. I had to be at the treatment center at 7:30 AM, but I had a wonderful send off. Around 6:00 AM our family from New Jersey walked through the door. They were sleepy, disheveled, and hungry, but they looked so good to this grandmother's eyes. It had been Christmas since we had seen the crew, and I wasn't sure Maia would be receptive to any advances I might make toward her. She had just awakened and looked at my bald head, smiled the biggest smile, and came right to my arms. She knew a soul sister when she saw one.

Gideon had slept all night in his car seat and was bright eyed and bushy tailed, ready to start his day. "Where are the toys, Gamma?" Tearing myself away from our daughter and her sugar-sweet family was tough, but chemo was calling.

As we waited to be called to the treatment room, I saw a lady out of the corner of my eye sit down and make room for someone else. Tom poked me and said, "Is that Karen?" Karen had been a member of our church, and her sons were friends with our boys at school. I stared across the room. Finally, bold Tom just came right out and asked, "Are you Karen Bing Mattingly?" She was.

Soon she was joined by her husband, Pank (nickname). Pank was there for his seventh chemo treatment for lung cancer. They caught it early, but he was being treated very aggressively. As it turned out, Pank and I were at the hospital at the same time the next day for our Neulasta shots, and he told me about his side effects following chemo. After hearing his long list of woes, I decided I didn't have anything to complain about. It seemed amazing to me what the body could take and still recover for more.

Once I got into the treatment room, I found a bed next to my chemo friend, Lisa. She was doing well and still very busy planning her daughter's wedding in June. Her husband was looking over a brochure about motorcycles. He told us he planned to buy one. It was the one topic of conversation Tom had difficulty sharing. Soon after my treatment started Glynnis Ballou showed up weighed down with gifts. I hadn't seen her since right after my surgery in October when she came to stay with me a couple of days during my recuperation. We had a lot of catching up to do. Trina and Gideon showed up for the event, and "Papa" Tom was more than willing to take Gideon around to show him off to all the other patients and nurses. Then Donna Gunnoe arrived, so we had quite a party going on.

To take advantage of having all the grand kids in town at the same time, we made an appointment to have professional photographs taken of the children. It was a mad house when we arrived at the studio because every man, woman, and child who happened to be in town for Easter had decided to have family pictures taken on Saturday. Our photographer was amazing. Working with five little ones wasn't easy, but of 30 shots, one had all the children looking reasonably comfortable with no one crying and no one making a silly face. I was so proud.

Late Saturday afternoon, I was doing some last-minute touches to my hair (wig) in preparation for evening services at church when the chemo symptoms started coming on. I was really shocked. It was a full 24 hours ahead of schedule. I made it through the service, and we hightailed it back to the house where I threw myself into preparing dishes for Easter dinner the next day. I felt like I was on a game show trying to beat the clock before my time ran out. "You can do this, Judy. You can do this. Get it done. Get it done." I kept repeating the phrase until I fell into bed.

EASTER

✿

I awoke to the precious sounds of little voices in the kitchen. Trina was assisting Gideon in the traditional egg coloring. I had planned to help, but chemo's side effects changed those plans. I could never have done the terrific job Trina did anyway. She used the store-bought dye and colored pens to make the most intricate designs. I was meant to stay in bed that morning.

People started arriving at the house around 2:30 in the afternoon. We had invited our son-in-law's immediate family and ours. Throughout the day, I rose and made a contribution to the festivities here and there then grudgingly got back into bed and drifted around the room in Percocet bliss.

The meal was grand with beef tenderloin, and baked ham thrown in for good measure. The salads, vegetables, and desserts (other than my coconut cake) were all brought in by our guests. The celebration turned out rather well. Joel, Trina, and Ken Sr. hid Trina's decorated eggs, and Gideon and Ethan had a ball looking for the hidden gems in the grass, bushes, and shrubs around the house.

In much need of peace and quiet, I eagerly bid everyone good-bye in the evening. Trina and Kenny went off to stay with Kenny's sister for a couple of days. They knew I wouldn't be up for pleasantries when Monday dawned. After they left, no one was there but Tom, me, and the pain. I decided I wanted them all to come back to take my mind off the slide of misery I was slipping down. It seemed so silly. First, I wanted them to go then I realized I needed them as psychological relief.

Monday, I spiraled into some of the most severe pain yet. It was worse from my knees down to my toes, but my shoulders and back, not to be left out, began to hurt as well.

I found it easier to sleep away the pain than to face it straight

on. I meditated on the e-mail my college roommate, Janice

Bradley, had sent the previous Monday in response to my

newsletter. I read it again, and my spirit soared with renewed

hope.

The comments were written by Ron Hutchcraft con-

cerning Paul and Silas and the experiences they endured in

Acts 16: They were "stripped, beaten . . . severely flogged, .

. . thrown into prison." Not only that, they were put "in the

inner cell" and their feet were "fastened in the stocks." You

would think that would have beaten the song out of them, but

no. They sang hymns to God in the midnight hour. Ron said,

"Not all prisons have physical walls. It's easy to get frus-

trated, self-pitying, negative or bitter. But you can choose,

as Paul did, to continue instead to enjoy your Lord; to still

make His music for others. In fact, people will listen to what

you have to say about Jesus because of what you're going

through. Your soul can be free, no matter how imprisoned the rest of you may be."

Later Paul said he was "hard pressed on every side, but not crushed; perplexed, but not in despair; . . . struck down, but not destroyed" (*2 Corinthians 4:8*). Nothing should stop us from hearing God's music or from playing God's music. The message was enough to get me through Monday, Tuesday, and Wednesday. It was enough when one of my fingernails broke and then split right down the middle. Then I looked at all my fingers and realized the nail beds had widened. I knew I was going to lose them all — even my toenails. I wondered if I could wrap them with rubber bands so they wouldn't disappear. It was a thought.

Then the numbness set in. I sensed it first in my right foot. It was in the ball and then spread out toward my toes. Then it took over my left foot, then my right hand, then my left, affecting my fingers. What was puzzling was the numbness in my upper lip and parts of my nose. The doctor had warned me this might happen, but I thought: No. I'm not

going to get every little side effect on the list. No! Regard-

less, the numbness was spreading. The doctor had told me to

let him know when this happened because if it wasn't treated

promptly, it could become permanent.

Before hitting the road to return to New Jersey, Kenny,

Trina, and the kids stopped by our house to gather some

last-minute items. I fed them spaghetti carbonara (a Gerdis-

family favorite), then with tears, I sent them on their way

to the East Coast. I walked back into the house after seeing

them disappear from Bluegrass Drive. I sighed and prayed

a prayer of thanksgiving, "Oh, Lord. Thank you for my

family and all my friends who have supported me through

this adventure with Scriptures, songs and Psalms. You are so

good, Lord."

The music is always there. You just have to listen!

WOE IS ME!

✸

The first Friday in May, I was scheduled to have blood work again and a private exam with one of the oncology nurses. I discussed the numbness that had taken over my fingers, the bottoms of my feet, my toes, my upper lip, and the lower part of my nose. Katie sighed and said, "You know, Judy, you have been through so much and have had so many side effects to deal with. When you come in next week for your treatment, you need to discuss this with the doctor. With all you've been through, they might allow you to opt out of your last treatment."

I couldn't believe what I was hearing. I could have a free pass? That was like the "get out of jail free" card. I contemplated what she said the rest of the week and decided that if the doctor could answer two major questions, I would go ahead, pass "Go," and head straight for home.

The day of my treatment, Tom and I arrived at 8:30 in the morning. I was surprised to see all my chemo buddies still sitting in the waiting room. Usually, they arrived ahead of me and were already in their beds, saving room for me in the middle of the pack. We began discussing why we had been allowed a little extra bed time and decided it was because of The Oaks (the fillies-only equivalent of The Kentucky Derby, which is always run the Friday before the famous horse race run the first Saturday every May). In fact, all morning and into the afternoon, the treatment center had their own versions of The Kentucky Oaks and The Kentucky Derby in the office hallways.

As Tom and I waited in the examination room, I was a little on edge because I was to meet a new oncologist. Would he be able to answer my questions? He arrived, and I had to restrain myself from laughing out loud. Why, it appeared he was barely dry behind the ears! Was this a joke? Doogie Howser was going to answer my questions? Let's get real! However, in his eyes, I saw such kindness. I asked him, "Have you read my records?"

He assured me he had read every single word and couldn't believe all I had been through. Such gentleness and empathy! I liked this guy. He asked me some questions; then it was my turn. I began, "I have experienced unusual numbness in my hands, feet, and lip. Will this next treatment of Taxol mean since this numbness is still with me, it will be twice as bad as the last time?"

His answer, "It could."

Second question: "Can you assure me if I have numbness again it will eventually go away?"

"No, I cannot." he replied. Well, that was to the point! Then he continued, "For some people, it subsides rather quickly, maybe within six or eight weeks after treatment. For others, it can last a year or so. And for some, it never goes away."

So I said, "Katie mentioned to me last week I could consider not having this last treatment, and I should discuss it with you before making a decision. I know there has to be a reason why eight treatments were prescribed for me. Can you tell me what you think?"

He explained eight was not necessarily a magic number, but in trials, eight treatments gave the most successful results. He said considering the type of cancer I had, it would be wise to take full advantage of the treatments recommended, which would diminish the likelihood of the cancer's returning. But, he also indicated I could opt out if I really wanted to. It was up to me.

Tom had heard the whole conversation, and I glanced over at him sitting against the wall. I asked him what he thought. His reply was, "Judy, you need to weigh the options here. Opt out and take a risk the cancer will return at some point, but you won't have the numbness. Take the treatment and know you have done everything you can to squash this thing but risk having numbness."

It seemed simple enough. I heard myself exclaim, "You heard him, Doc!"

Making a concession, the doctor offered to instruct the nurses to give me a lesser dose. Rather than the 2 1/2-hour Taxol drip, I would get 30 minutes lopped off the session. So the grand total treatment time with premeds, flushes, and other drips would be six hours, not the normal six and a half.

I was the first of my chemo buddies to arrive in the treatment area, so I claimed beds for all my friends who arrived shortly thereafter. For Lisa, it was to be her last treatment too. She privately admitted to me she had almost opted out as well, but not for the same reasons. She just had had enough. She had breast cancer when she was 28 years old and begged the doctors to take both her breasts at that time. They told her it was too drastic a step for someone so young. "Oh, Judy, if they had only listened to me, I wouldn't be lying in this bed right now with Stage IV cancer in my gut. I can't get that out of my mind."

Mid morning, Donna Gunnoe arrived with Panera Bread quiches and pink roses for Lisa and me. It was a celebration day! Right before I left, one of the nurses brought me a card signed by all the medical staff in the treatment room. They had each written a special note of encouragement.

Everything was set up for the radiation examinations and tattoos for the following two weeks at a clinic in Frankfort, but the actual treatments wouldn't begin until later in June. I thought it would be convenient and such a blessing to go straight from my radiation treatment to work — both in the same town.

As I looked at my hands I could tell it would be only a matter of time before I lost all my finger nails. They were loosening away from the nail beds, and it was a strange sight. I spoke with my insurance company's medical counselor who insisted I needed to take the polish off so my nails could "breathe." When I did, I could see my nails were turning black and blue. They looked as though I had hit them with a hammer. I decided they didn't need to breathe after all, so I covered them up again with nail polish. If they were going to fall off anyway, they might as well look their best until their untimely death. With the buckling, all it would take would be a little bump, tug, or pull and — adios! Looking at my toenails, I could tell they might fall to the same fate. Wearing close-toed shoes became agony, so I began wearing open-toed sandals, glad it was spring and soon to be summer so my "little piggies" wouldn't freeze.

Due to the steroids I was taking, my tear ducts began to leak. What a nuisance! Tears would fall, and my nose would drip without provocation. I began carrying a tissue with me at all times, apologizing to customers and friends whenever the waterworks started. Because of the numbness, however, sometimes I wouldn't be aware tears and/or snot were dripping down my cheeks and onto my lip.

Saturday evening, after my Friday treatment, the pain started again. It began in my back then moved into my shoulders. I knew the next day my feet, legs and knees would hurt, *but* it would be the last time. Alleluia!

PART III

GETTING TO THE
OTHER SIDE

☸

THROUGH THE STORM

※

By the end of May, I had my first meeting with the oncology radiologist in Frankfort. If anything, he was quite thorough. Taking a lot of time, he explained all the ramifications of radiation, giving me odds and percentages that left me reeling. I had thought the radiation would be a snap. After our discussion, I began to doubt. He certainly gave me a lot to ponder. Trying to impress on me the importance of my receiving radiation, he explained without radiation, there would be a 38 percent chance the kind of cancer I had would return. With radiation, the odds dropped to 8 percent.

That seemed like good news. The bad news was because the area to be treated was only a layer of skin and a few ribs away from my right lung, I would risk damaging that organ.

The effects can take various forms: one is a serious type of

pneumonia that can appear during treatment or many months

afterward. At the first sign of coughing, congestion, or dif-

ficulty breathing, I was to contact him immediately. Another

organ in close proximity to the radiation site is the heart. One

positive was the treatments would focus on my right side,

and the heart is situated center and to the left of the body.

I had been told by my oncologist my treatments would

last six weeks, and I probably would not experience the

burns I had 13 years previously. Unfortunately, according

to the radiologist, I had been misled. He made it very clear

toward the end of my *seven*-week treatment (every week day

for seven weeks), I might not even be capable of working

but might need to return home and sit in front of a fan to get

relief. Then he added, "I will try to keep the burning to a

minimum, so as not to create scarring."

"Scarring?" I murmured. "What are you talking about?"

I wasn't expecting his reply, "Oh, you've seen people who have been severely burned, haven't you? Well, that is what I mean by radiation scarring."

Upon examination of my chest wall, he stood back and said, "Oh, this is good. This is very good. I can't say I've ever seen such a clear outline of the previous radiation."

Puzzled, I said, "Why is that so good?"

He explained, "Radiation in and unto itself causes cancer. It is a very slight chance — about half a percent — and you definitely don't want radiation cancer. (He shuddered). It is one of the worst types of cancer with a high mortality rate. When we give additional radiation treatments it is important to try to stay away from any areas of the body that have received radiation before because if we overlap, the odds of getting radiation cancer increase dramatically. You show a very slight shadow, indicating the margins of your previous treatment. I can definitely see the areas to avoid. I've never seen this before."

I thought, *Well, thank you, Lord, for a ray of sunshine in this gloomy monolog!*

The radiologist mentioned other side effects could be lethargy, extreme tiredness, and swelling of my arm where the lymph nodes had been taken. When I really thought about the scarring possibilities, I concluded it wouldn't matter much in light of all the scars already there. As I questioned the doctor further, he indicated they would be monitoring me carefully, and possible radiation effects are either a dry burn or a wet burn. He also promised if I showed a tendency toward a wet burn, which was important to avoid, treatment would be suspended until I had recovered enough to continue.

As I left the office, I glanced at my fingernails. They were still hanging on, but they smelled to high heaven. The only thing I could liken the odor to was rotting flesh. I began flushing my nails with hydrogen peroxide twice a day, but nothing seemed to eliminate the smell. I knew I had encountered that specific odor once before, and it finally dawned on me it was when Mary Burnett had shown me the tumors on her chest.

I found a pair of shoes that would allow my toes to stick way out from the straps. I was so thrilled, I ordered two more pairs in other colors. It is amazing how we can adjust to just about any circumstance the Lord allows to come our way.

On my way home from the radiology appointment, I remembered again the Scripture in Matthew that states that Jesus "MADE" the disciples get into the boat and go to the other side" of the lake. I'm sure they could see the storm clouds rolling in and knew it was going to be a bumpy, dangerous voyage. But Jesus MADE them get in the boat. When my adventure began, I'm not sure if I had known just how stormy this journey would become I would have been so willing to jump in the boat, but I knew HE was right there in the boat with me through all the challenges I'd overcome. He walked the path with me, holding my hand as I made my way through the cancer cyclone. Feeling His presence so close made enduring the storm worth it all.

I was reminded of a story about a young woman driving along with her father. They came up on a storm. The young woman asked her father what she should do. He said, "Keep driving." Cars began to pull over to the side, and the storm got worse.

"What should I do?" the young woman asked again.

"Keep on driving." her father replied.

Ahead a few feet she noticed 18 wheelers were pulling over. She told her dad, "I must pull over, because I can barely see ahead! It is terrible out here! Everyone is pulling over." Her father told her to not give in but to just keep driving.

The storm was raging on all sides, but she never stopped driving, and soon she could see a little more clearly. After a couple of miles, creeping along at a slow pace, she emerged onto dry land, and the sun came out. Her father said, "Now, pull over and get out."

She said, "But why now?"

He said, "Get out and look back at all the people who gave up and are still in the storm. You never gave up, and now your storm is over."

What a testimony for anyone who might be going through something big. Just because others, even those who appear to be the strongest, give up, you don't have to. Just keep on going. Up ahead, your storm will soon be over, and the sun will shine on your face again. So, I determined in my heart to just keep going. I had no idea how the storm would worsen to the point my doctor, not me, would give up.

GIVING THANKS

E ven in the depths of misery, when the dark clouds overshadowed my thoughts, I couldn't forget the member of our family battling her heart problems. Maia was never far from my thoughts or my prayers. The end of February, she had a checkup indicating a decline in her weight, and all signs pointed to the need to have another valvuloplasty when she was six months old.

We were constantly in touch with our New Jersey family to hear about every milestone and all the grand antics our grandchildren were doing. In May, Maia was due to have her first appointment with the pediatric cardiologist in three months. We weren't sure what the news would be, but we had been praying a major turnaround in her condition would be forthcoming.

Not only did Kenny and Trina have to constantly be alert to any changes in Maia's health, but they were dealing with insurance issues as well. The business manager at the doctor's office where Maia received her care and checkups was adamant the money paid through their health-care insurance was insufficient, and they would owe an exorbitant amount each time they saw the doctor. After investigating the situation, Kenny had discovered the office manager was charging for a service they weren't even receiving, which explained why his insurance was reluctant to fork over the extra money. When they pointed out the discrepancy to the manager, she said even though they weren't receiving the special examination, by New Jersey law, they were allowed to charge for it anyway.

Their May visit to the pediatric cardiologist required two steps of faith: (1) faith the Lord would somehow see to it the doctor and the insurance company would agree on a settlement, and (2) faith Maia had improved enough that the predicted surgery would not be needed.

The doctor's exam revealed Maia still had the hole in her heart, but it measured exactly the same as it had in February. Because Maia had grown, her heart had grown as well, meaning the hole — even though the same size — was deemed to be smaller in relation to the size of her heart. In addition, her chest pressure had gone down. It was wonderful news since babies with HRHS have a lot of pressure in their hearts due to narrow pathways and tight valves. Additionally, her weight had increased enough to bring a smile to the doctor's face. Previously, Maia had not kept up with the growth charts used to measure her improvement. Her strength abilities remained good as well. She had always been a bit of a super girl, evidenced by her holding her head up when she was only about two weeks old and grabbing people's fingers with a death grip. At the appointment, she kept snatching the ultrasound instrument from the doctor's hands. The doctor's conclusion? Maia would not need the valvuloplasty procedure at six months. She was scheduled for another appointment three months later.

"The LORD is my strength and my shield; my HEART trusts in Him, and I am helped. My HEART leaps for joy and I will give thanks to Him in song." *Psalm 28:7*

Just about the time we thought things were going so well, a fly dropped into our soup! I was at home when a friend, Jim Bickley, called to say he was rushing Tom to the emergency room. He wasn't sure what was happening, but he suspected Tom might be having a stroke. They had been having lunch in downtown Louisville; when Tom was unable to retrieve his credit card from his wallet to pay for his meal. Jim realized Tom was displaying classic signs of a stroke and insisted on driving him to the hospital.

I got to the hospital in record time, and they ushered me into the ER cubical. Tom seemed in good spirits, and he related how frustrating it had been to focus on doing such a simple task as paying for his meal and not be able to make his hands do what his mind was directing. They kept him in the hospital for two days, running tests and administering physical therapy to his left arm and hand. When he was released, he was instructed to not work for a couple of days. The doctors prescribed Plavix and an aspirin regimen and ordered him to whittle down his waist size by about four inches.

As soon as Tom returned to work, my dear friend, Yvonne, arrived for her annual visit from up-state New York. It had been almost a year since we'd been together because I received my cancer diagnosis about the time of year I usually visited her in Portville. We had a fantastic time doing what we do best: shopping, talking, watching movies, eating, shopping, talking and watching movies. Having her with me was even more special because she was engaged to be married in September, and I got to help her select the perfect dress for her wedding. It was a week of rejoicing after many years praying God would send the perfect man into her life.

I have to admit the "shopping" part was exhausting. Many moments I had to stop and catch my breath, and we laughed at the old expression "shop until you drop." I seemed to be dropping much sooner than in years past, but, it was good to experience a semblance of normalcy. It had been much too long.

The second evening of Yvonne's visit, I was buttoning my pajamas when I felt the nail on my left index finger pull back to the quick. I felt sick to my stomach as carefully Yvonne lifted up the nail. It was hanging on by a small cuticle thread. I hesitated to pull it off altogether for fear it would bleed, so I placed a bandage over the tip, and I wore it for a couple of days. Later while we were in a clothing store, Yvonne reached down and picked up something off the floor. She said, "Judy, here is your bandage." I looked at my finger and saw the nail had come off completely. It didn't look as ugly or unsightly as I had feared. In fact, a small portion of a new nail had already begun to grow in, which is probably why the nail had come off. I debated about what I would do when I lost all the nails. Should I get some gloves, wear little bandages on all my finger tips or just manage without?

QUESTIONS, QUESTIONS

W hen I saw my oncologist again, I presented him with the discouraging side effects the radiologist had spelled out two weeks earlier. I hoped he might be as dismayed as I had been and suggest I go to another doctor for my treatments. My hope was dashed when he agreed that because I no longer had breast tissue to shield my lungs, heart, and rib cage, the radiation could be damaging. He even added that ribs can crack from exposure to radiation. He also confirmed he had seen women with intense scaring from radiation burns.

Tom and I talked about this, and I finally just had to leave it in God's hands. I wasn't sure why it upset me so much since I was already scarred from the surgeries. What difference would it make?

The medical line of defense to prevent the cancer's return would be a new drug called Arimidex. It is the latest hormone drug for this purpose. Tamoxifen was the most common drug used in past years, but the new drug is more effective at preventing the return of my type of cancer — especially in my age group. The side effects would be hot flashes, nausea, decreased energy, weakness, pain, back pain, bone pain, and increased coughing. Joint pain and stiffness have been reported as well. I will be taking the pill every day for at least five years, and perhaps the rest of my life. The doctor made an appointment for me to return in 30 days to see how well I tolerated the new medication.

A question had haunted me for the past months: how would I know if the cancer had returned? I can no longer have mammograms to detect cancer cells. When I posed this question to the doctor, he said that if it returns, it will show up in the bones, the liver or the brain. He further explained if I experience any persistent bone pain, other than in joints, I would need to contact his office as soon as possible. If I experience unexplained nausea, it could be in the liver. If I have bouts of confusion, disorientation, dizziness, or severe headaches, it could be in the brain. Bouts of confusion, you say? That might be a tough one to identify.

As I rode back home in the car I thought about a friend from work, a cancer survivor, (one of the 1 percent of men who have survived breast cancer). Since returning from a hiking trip, he had been complaining of pain in his upper leg. I called him immediately. He had just come home from the hospital after his leg broke while trying to get up from a seated position. It was breast cancer reappearing in his bone. He was in high spirits, saying he would be going through radiation at the same time and the same place where I would be getting my treatments in Frankfort. We were going to be radiation buddies.

Within three weeks of probing the doctor with my questions, I learned of two more friends who'd had recurrences. One was six years out, and one was seven years out from breast cancer. So there was evidence of the reality of the disease: my friend with the bone cancer, another friend with liver cancer, and still another with brain cancer. That can rock your security, but I needed to realize nothing is "for sure" when it comes to cancer, and I had to trust Him to care for all that concerned me about cancer and its unknown. I can't wait to see what the Father's good plans are for me.

"'DEM OLD COTTON FIELDS BACK HOME"

✸

B efore starting on my radiation regime, Tom and I decided to drive to Arkansas for my 45th high-school reunion in Hot Springs. I had graduated from a consolidated school on the outskirts of Hot Springs in 1967.

The first place we visited was Hillcrest Children's Home off Malvern Road. My father had been the Home's administrator from 1957 until 1967. In those days, more than 100 children were housed in six dorms or cottages. The campus looked very different as we pulled up the steep drive and parked for a moment outside the administration building. I lost count of the number of cottages dotting the landscape.

They even had an indoor swimming pool! We didn't see any of the 40 or so children who live there now. Perhaps they were all off-site on vacation, but it was nice to see where I had spent the most formative years of my life and the chapel where Tom and I had our first kiss.

To get to the Lake Hamilton area for the reunion, we drove a familiar route. I call it "the country lane" of Golf Links Road. In the fall of 1966, Tom had driven down State Highway 7, a dangerously curvy route from Springfield, Missouri, through the Ozark Mountains, to pay me a visit. On our first date, we decided to go into the "city," which we could reach either by the country road or the city road (Malvern Road). I decided we would go the more scenic country route, leaving Malvern Road for our return.

In those days, sewage was often dumped into rivers and streams, which made for an interesting odor seeping out and over the highways and byways. I didn't think anything about the bridge we crossed, which spanned a country creek, until Tom looked over at me, smiled wryly, and said "That's okay."

I thought about what he said for a second, not understanding *what* was okay. Then suddenly I realized he thought I had made the stink in the car. I was livid with embarrassment yelling, "That wasn't me! It was the creek!"

He, being a Connecticut Yankee, responded, "Is that what they call it down here?"

How dare him! No fine, upstanding, Southern boy would ever accuse a lady of such an indiscretion!

Fast forward 42 years. It was with great anticipation we approached the "creek" bridge. We rolled down the windows and took a good whiff. Of course, no odor was being emitted. The creek was pristine. Not only that, the city had constructed a beautiful walking path alongside the bubbling brook running several miles upstream. Times . . . they had changed.

Most people don't know Hot Springs is quite a tourist area. There are three main lakes, Lake Catherine, Lake Hamilton, and Lake Ouachita (pronounced Wa-chee-ta). The last has over 900 miles of shoreline. We ambled by Oaklawn Park Racetrack where my dad used to sneak behind the backside fence line to watch the horses run during the spring meet. Then we inched our way down Central Avenue in bumper-to-bumper traffic, past Bathhouse Row, and the headquarters for Mountain Valley Spring Water. People were lugging their buckets and jugs to collect the hot water bubbling up out of the ground. It was good to see some things hadn't changed. Luxurious auction houses used to sit across from the bathhouses, where Tom and I had gone on our first date, but those were no longer in business.

Hot Springs is a national park, and it was an ideal place for me to grow up as a teenager. I wasn't allowed to go to dances or movies as a youngster, fortunately the area offered many other things for a dating couple to do. Situated between two towering mountains, it was the epitome of natural beauty

and offered untold hiking paths, scenic vistas, rock climbing,

and swimming-holes.

We wound our way up West Mountain and stopped at two

of the lookout posts, taking in the spectacular views of the

bustling city, lakes, and countryside. West Mountain was the

favorite "parking" spot for young couples in my day. I guess

today's youth have to go to the lake for "submarine races"

because signs were posted that the mountain road closed at

sundown. Before descending the mountain, we called my

best friend from high school, Juanice, to let her know we

were heading toward McClard's where she and her husband,

Jerry, would meet us for a dinner of the best barbeque west

of the Mississippi.

We ended up practicing gluttony that evening. We stuffed

our faces with all manner of goodies: brisket, ribs, and hot

tamales. McClard's was Bill Clinton's favorite restaurant, so

pictures of "ole Bill" were on practically every wall, and I half expected to see him stroll in at any moment. He gradu-

ated the same year, 1964, I did, but not from Lakeside. He

went to Central High, the big-city school. I did march in

parades with Bill, but I don't recall ever meeting him per-

sonally.

Juanice and Jerry live in a little town, Royal, consisting

of a post office, a couple of churches, and farmland adjacent

to Lake Ouachita. Their home is off the main road by a half

mile and is nestled among tall pines next to a creek with

pasture land approaching their back patio. It had all the com-

forts of country living and was where deer and buffalo roam.

Well . . . maybe not buffalo, but deer, horses, and turkeys,

as well as one or two snakes, make their homes around their

beautiful spread. It was just what the doctor ordered for my

respite from cancer treatments. The peace and quiet settled

my weary soul.

A good number of former classmates showed up Sat-

urday morning at the "old" Lakeside High School gym. We

had a nice tour of the modern, present-day facilities. Then later in the evening, we met for barbeque at a clubhouse on Lake Hamilton where we ate, talked, and laughed until we were all talked out. For dessert, they served cake with pink ribbons and pink balloons to honor my cancer fight.

When I had initially called Juanice to tell her we would be coming to the reunion, I told her we wanted to stay over Sunday morning and attend church services with them before heading home to Kentucky. I knew many of the people at the First Baptist Church of Royal had been praying for both me and Maia the last several months. I wanted to have a chance to thank them for their faithfulness.

As we packed for the trip, Tom had asked if he should include a suit and tie. I told him it wouldn't be necessary because on Sunday we would be attending a country church, and I doubted people dressed up very much. We packed casual attire. When we got up Sunday morning, Jerry had already left since he would be teaching an adult class, and he needed to prepare for leading worship as their song director. I noticed Juanice seemed to be dressed quite well in high heels, a lovely blouse, and pearls. I began to wonder if I was dressed appropriately.

At church we were ushered back to a fellowship hall where all the adult classes met prior to Sunday school. It was a great time for snacks and coffee. Everyone looked so festive! I think I even commented to one of the ladies how spring-like they appeared. Then it was time for Juanice to introduce us. Her back was to me as she began by telling them I was the one they had been lifting up in prayer for nine months. Then she turned to look at me, and I noticed she had tears streaming down her cheeks. She said, "Judy, I don't know if you've noticed, but everyone here is wearing pink today in honor of you." I gasped and looked around. Sure enough, everyone was wearing different shades and hues of pink. Even the men! There were pink shirts, pink ties, pink dresses, and pink blouses. I burst into tears. I couldn't remember ever being so honored and loved. After our class, we walked into the sanctuary, and the choir streamed onto the platform. All of them were dressed in pink. It was almost more than my heart could take in. I was truly blessed.

NAIL BITES

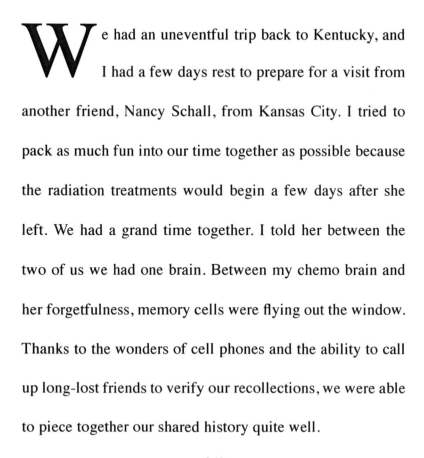

W e had an uneventful trip back to Kentucky, and I had a few days rest to prepare for a visit from another friend, Nancy Schall, from Kansas City. I tried to pack as much fun into our time together as possible because the radiation treatments would begin a few days after she left. We had a grand time together. I told her between the two of us we had one brain. Between my chemo brain and her forgetfulness, memory cells were flying out the window. Thanks to the wonders of cell phones and the ability to call up long-lost friends to verify our recollections, we were able to piece together our shared history quite well.

When Yvonne was with me, my left index fingernail came off. When Nancy arrived, my right pinky nail fell off. A few days later, I looked at my hand, and saw my left thumb nail hanging by a thread. I finally settled in my mind that I would be losing them all. I remembered how adamant I had been about not losing those fingernails. It was interesting how time and tears changed my outlook. Early on, I had felt that losing my nails would be even more difficult than losing my hair, but when faced with the inevitable, I just accepted it unafraid, knowing I would be safe in the Father's hands no matter what the circumstances.

The day arrived when I had only two fingernails remaining: the index finger and ring finger of my right hand. I actually thought those would be the first to go, but they hung on with tenacity. My index nail never was much to look at anyway because it was smashed in a car door and nearly torn off when I was four or five years old in Fairbanks, Alaska. A feisty little boy had raced me to the car, and when I reached out to stop him from slamming the door, my finger got in the way. I saw stars through my tears of pain, but through the years I had treasured the crazy-looking finger and nail. Wouldn't you know it would be the last one to hang on tight? I started bandaging each bare and gruesome digit to not frighten anyone who might happen to glance at my unkempt finger tips. My middle fingers were the worst, looking every bit as if a school of flesh-eating minnows had gnawed away the skin. It was an ugly sight. Jayna Jamison, a friend from church, gave me two pairs of the most delicate cotton dress gloves that had been handed down in her family. They were treasured heirlooms and so fine I hesitated wearing them for fear I'd get a speck of dirt or grime on the white, ivory sleeves. I wore them to church on occasion.

Knowing when to wrap my fingers with bandages was a problem. If I knew I would be getting my hands wet, I delayed the tedious unwrapping, stretching, and wrapping the strips again. Water would render the bandages useless with the fibers fraying and ending up making me look a bit like Edward Scissorhands with strings hanging helter-skelter. I came up with a brilliant plan one day as I prepared two dishes for a July 4 cookout. I remembered Micah had brought a big bag of surgical gloves for Gideon and Ethan to blow up and play with one Christmas. I found them stashed away in a drawer in the family room. They worked just fine, protecting my fingers from the mess of chopping and mixing the ingredients for my famous peanut-butter pie. The tedious task of shuffling through papers, turning the pages of a book, or delicately retrieving change from my wallet exasperated me to the nth degree. I wondered if I might not need occupational therapy to master the new skills needed to just cope with everyday living.

BLESSED "INSURANCE"

❂

The end of June, I was called into the corporate office for a meeting with my employer. Thinking I would be given new pricing for some of the homes I was selling, instead I found out my company would be dropping my insurance effective August 1. What a blow! They assured me they had done some work on my behalf, getting in touch with representatives of my insurance company to see what my options would be. I had two: (1) To continue with my current company with a single policy for $1500 a month due to a "pre-existing condition," or (2) To apply to a state program, which could not deny coverage, for a mere $800 a month. I was shocked!

I quickly filled out all the necessary paperwork and started the waiting process to hear if I would qualify for the state coverage. With any new policy, I would have to start the policy year over, owing $2,000, with an additional $1,500 deductible, plus two months of premiums. I calculated I would owe $5,100 by the end of August. My head and my wallet hurt.

In the meantime, I approached my radiology oncologist about the treatments to see if we could work out something since the existing schedule had me receiving radiation into the second week of August. The doctor was very understanding — calculating and recalculating — to come up with a plan that would increase my radiation dosage each day, thus giving me the recommended treatments needed to curtail the possible spread of cancer in a shorter time frame. Increasing the radiation, of course, meant the redness and burning would be more intense and would occur more quickly. It also meant

I might not be able to continue working through the course of the treatments as I had planned.

This new course of events provided another opportunity to trust that God knew what He was doing in my life. In *Isaiah 49:16*, I read that He had engraved me on the palms of His hand. I preferred to think that He *tattooed* me there. Whether by name or portrait, I would be there forever . . . never to be erased . . . just like the tattoos on my chest the radiologist uses to direct the cancer-killing rays. A tattoo is about as permanent a mark as one can get. Just thinking about God tattooing me into His palm brought a smile — I was loved that much!

In July, I got a call from the insurance representative assigned to my case asking me to send him a fax with the following statement: *I would like to go with the state continuation policy effective 8/1/09.* I asked, "What is this about?"

He indicated he was trying to get me enrolled in the new state plan that continues an employee's existing policy for

18 months after being dropped by their employer. I asked what the price would be, but he hesitated to answer. He didn't want to get my hopes up if he couldn't convince them to transfer me over to the new plan. "Trust me, it is much, much less than the $800 state plan."

I quickly sent out an emergency plea for all my friends to bombard heaven on my behalf. I had decided if I hadn't heard anything about my insurance by Wednesday, I would call. However, the next Monday I received a new insurance card in the mail, so I assumed I had been accepted into the "continuing" coverage at the lower rate. Tuesday, when I called my agent to verify, he assured me that was probably not going to be the case and, again, not to get my hopes up. He had talked to a number of people who were very discouraging about my chances. Only one had suggested there was hope. He mentioned he would be mailing off my application for the state plan on Wednesday, saying, "Judy, it does not look at all hopeful."

I went to my treatment Thursday morning and stopped by my office to fax a medical bill to my AFLAC agent. For some reason it would not fax, and I struggled for an undue amount of time, becoming very frustrated in my efforts. As I worked on the fax, my office phone rang. When I looked at the caller ID it showed my insurance company's name. I picked up the receiver and heard my agent, "Well, I have good news."

I yelled, "You're kidding!"

He said, "No. I'm not kidding. Everywhere I turned I was being denied. Finally I went to the top of the ladder. I sat down and told them I knew you didn't qualify under normal circumstances but your situation was not normal, and I wanted them to make an exception. They agreed."

Of course, I was ecstatic. I told him I loved him over and over. He laughed and said that made two, me and his wife who was seven months pregnant. He said that was one reason he had tried so hard because he just couldn't imagine what it would do to their family if they lost their insurance.

I had just told my friend, Juanice, in Arkansas the insurance thing had to be at the top of my prayer list, and she had assured me she would be mentioning it to all the women at Royal Baptist Church. I couldn't wait to tell her to send out the bulletin.

Later, I came to realize just how miraculous it was for me to have a continuation of my insurance. The first person with whom I shared the good news was Shantha Diaz, who works for my insurance company. She was absolutely giddy with delight when she heard. At one point she said she had thought about calling and talking with the agent working with me on the extension, but each time she felt a check in her spirit. No, the Lord was in charge, and He would handle things on my behalf. She didn't need to meddle. Then I called Brenda, a pew-mate from church whose job it is to help people losing their coverage or trying to find coverage. She told me in all her years of working, she had never heard of anyone getting a continuation like I did without either losing their job or being laid off.

RESTORATION

✸

By the end of July, my hair had started growing in by centimeters, giving me a little bit of a Jamie Lee Curtis style. It was salt and pepper and didn't look half bad. The gray wig had prepared me for the new color. My eyebrows were another story. They weren't quite what I had before cancer. They appeared as a fuzzy bundle of faint gray. My eyelashes started to sprout. The problem was, though, they didn't grow in at the same rate, so they more or less looked like a bar graph for the stock market. The hair thing was certainly taking its time returning to normal all the way around. My last chemo treatment was May 1, and I had thought within three months I would see more progress.

Tom and I had to go to a Rotary dinner at one of the country clubs in Louisville. We pulled up and parked in the lot out front. Before exiting the car I thought I'd best look things over in the visor mirror. I pulled the flap down and checked my hair, my eyebrows, eyelashes, nose, etc. Then I spotted them! How did that happen? It couldn't be! There, growing out about an inch was not one, not two, but three chin hairs! Now that's pathetic! The top of my head can only produce a centimeter, but my chin can grow a whole crop? Something was wrong with that picture. It was a good thing I carried tweezers in my purse, or I would have just stayed in the car.

All my fingernails eventually fell off. I had one remaining when Glynnis Ballou stopped by one day. I put out my finger so she could see the last one, and there it was, sticking out and away from the nail bed, ready to fly the coop. With my other hand, I pulled it off and tossed it way. Later in the evening I was restlessly turning under a throw while watching

TV in the family room. I kept feeling a poking, stabbing pain in my toe and foot. When I rose from the chair, a toenail was on the floor, and my big toe was bare.

The numbness in my hands and fingers finally subsided, but the same couldn't be said for my toes and the soles of my feet. I had to learn to live with the strangeness of having no feeling. I had to be mindful not to turn suddenly and be careful when I started to walk after sitting for long periods of time. When asked what it felt like, I told people it was as though I had on heavy woolen socks that had scrunched down in my shoe, leaving me with a wad of fabric to walk on. The same was true when I wore sandals.

As the nail shedding began, on my Facebook page Trina jokingly asked how I intended to pick my nose once all my fingernails were gone. Surprisingly, it wasn't a problem. Do you know what was? Itching! Now that was frustrating. How do you scratch an itch when you don't have nails? I tried to keep something handy to accomplish that all-important task, but more often than not I was stranded without a tool and would have to scrounge around for something to meet the need.

I continued to drive into Frankfort every weekday morning for my radiation treatments. One day the nurse looked at my chest wall and said she thought the doctor needed to see what was happening. He came in and said, "At the risk of sounding sadistic, this is what we want to see. It will get worse, Judy, but it has to." He went on to say even after my treatments ended, I would continue to burn, explaining it was much like a water hose: when you turn the spigot off, water continues to flow. He described my chest as a *brisk erythema*. I kept asking him to repeat the word, and I rolled it over my tongue several times to get the feel of the vowels and consonants and willing them to come out in a fluid manner.

Finally I said, "Do you want to know what I call it?"

They both said, "What?"

I said, "A world of hurt." And they laughed.

A few days later I told the crew I thought I was at the point where I might need prescription medication to handle the pain. The doctor was called in again to examine me. He said I wasn't quite there yet. What? I was no longer pink. I wasn't even red. I was a genuine *purple*, and the doctor was telling me it had to get worse before he would prescribe medication?

I always went into a little closet to don a hospital gown (open in the front) and pad my way back to the radiation treatment room. Once resting on the table, arms extended over my head, and the gown pulled back, they would start lining up all the little tattoos and zapping rays. I had become so familiar with the routine it wasn't a big deal anymore. All my modesty had fled.

Once, I came close to walking out of the changing room without the gown on at all! I caught myself at the last moment. I told the nurses what I had come close to doing, and they told the doctor. Usually he was rather dower and seldom smiled. I was shocked when he entered into a supposition about women who venture out in public with their breasts bared and their subsequent arrest for indecent exposure, but he had often wondered what would happen if a woman who had a bilateral mastectomy bared her chest. Would it be called indecent exposure? She would be no more exposed than any man would be and in some cases, less exposed. We were all left wondering the same thing. Now you know what is discussed behind the doctor's closed door. Things that make you go, "Hummmmm."

I may not have been at the point where I needed to have medication prescribed, but I was definitely at the point where I needed to wear as little as possible as soon as I got home from work. I would lather on the salve, creams, and lotions, and then slip on a light cotton, free-flowing gown. Finally, the doctor gave approval for me to take a Vicodin each evening to help me get through the night.

Approaching the end of my radiation, I could see the brilliant light at the end of the tunnel drawing closer. I was ready for it all to end. I was very grateful an area about two inches around my mastectomy scar was totally numb. It was a tremendous blessing especially since the last radiation blasts would focus along the bilateral incision. The total area of burn was a perfect 9-in. x 9-in. square, much larger than I had anticipated. The burn was so deep the technicians who prepared me before each treatment would try to stand away from my chest because the emanating heat caused them discomfort. It caused THEM discomfort? When I tried to put on a cool gel pack (a paper gel strip about 8 in. x 10 in. that I kept in the refrigerator) it would lose its cool power and be completely warm within 30 seconds. Finally, I couldn't work anymore. My assistant offered to take care of things at the office, and my boss encouraged me to just stay home for a couple of weeks.

I called ahead to the radiologist's office to ask the nurses if they could remove the traces of salve and lotions for me before my next treatment because it had become too painful to do it myself. They didn't like hearing that, so they scheduled an exam with the doctor before the next zapping. He came into the examination room and looked stunned at the amount of discoloration, blistering, and peeling that had begun. He didn't want to give me another treatment until I healed a little bit. The doctor ordered a Domeboro soak, which consisted of dissolving a solution in warm water, tearing gauze bandages into thin strips, soaking them in the solution, then placing them across my chest. Then they put a towel over the gauze and left me to soak for 30 minutes. Before leaving the office, I was given a week's supply. I was told to administer the soaks four times a day, follow with Silver Sulfadiazine Cream, which had the consistency of diaper-rash cream. I had to go to the office every day, so they could monitor the burns and decide when to continue the treatments.

Before I left his office, the doctor looked at me and said, "I'm mystified by you." I asked him what he meant, and he said, "Well, you are one strong lady. I've had many patients over the years who, when they got to this point in the treatment (third-degree burns), would go into depression and have a very difficult time handling what was happening to their bodies. You have such a positive attitude. It is amazing to me."

I just looked at him and said, "Doctor, I call it 'the grace of God'. I have hundreds of people all over the world who are praying for me. At any given time, I know someone is lifting me up to my Father, and because of His love and mercy toward me, I can find the strength to go on." He just shook his head and walked out of the room.

A dear friend, Fred Eicher, was a special source of inspiration during the many months of treatment. It seemed the Lord purposefully brought people back into my life from my past who had been long lost to me. Fred brought a box of latex gloves to me at church, and they were very handy for chores around the kitchen, laundry, and then for administering the salves. More than anything, though, Fred sent me the most uplifting music. In addition, he repeatedly brought The Word alive for me to ponder during the most troubling times. It was during the worst of the radiation that he sent me Scriptures about restoration. They were real faith builders.

" 'Now put it back into your cloak,' he said. So Moses put his hand back into his cloak, and when he took it out, it was restored, like the rest of his flesh." *Exodus 4:7*

"Then the king said to the man of God, 'Intercede with the LORD your God and pray for me that my hand may be restored.' So the man of God interceded with the LORD, and the king's hand was restored and became as it was before." *1 Kings 13:6*

". . . then his flesh is renewed like a child's; it is restored as in the days of his youth." *Job 33:25*

"Then he said to the man, 'Stretch out your hand.' So he stretched it out and it was completely restored, just as sound as the other." *Matthew 12:13*

"And the God of all grace, who called you to his eternal glory in Christ, after you have suffered a little while, will himself restore you and make you strong, firm and stead-fast." *1 Peter 5:10*

"STRONGER THAN I EVER KNEW"

I checked in at the radiologist's office every day, but the doctor wouldn't let them give me a treatment. Each day, he would shake his head and say, "I can't risk burn upon burn. Not today, maybe tomorrow." At the end of the week he said, "I will see you next Tuesday, and then we will determine if we should go ahead with the last five blast sessions or discontinue radiation altogether."

I had had a nice rest from the rays. I started to see a noticeable difference. Healing had begun, but where the skin had peeled, a raw, red, and blistered area remained, and I was not in favor of zapping it anytime soon. I wasn't sure what to expect when I went in for the consultation. Reta Stivers and Linda Igleheart took me to Frankfort for the appointment. I thought it interesting, since they were the ones with me when I heard the news 10 months earlier that my situation was going to be more serious than we had originally thought.

The doctor took one look, and I could tell he was pleased with what he saw. I braced myself for a pronouncement the radiation would continue, but I heard him say, "I think we should stop here. I don't want to do further damage. If we continue we would risk one of two things: (1) Such severe burns scaring would be a certainty and/or (2) Irritating the raw areas to such a degree infection would set in. When that happens, sometimes there is a propensity for the skin to fight healing. You could end up with open wounds for months, maybe even years."

His last words of advice were that I shouldn't pick at the peeling skin. He said it would be better if it just came off naturally because if I tried to hurry up the process I could remove new skin along with the old. When I told Trina, she said, "Oh, Mom, that is going to be so difficult for you because we are a very picky family!" When people came to the house, I would show them the burns if they cared to see them. One friend gasped, "Judy it looks just like the burn patients I used to treat in the hospital."

A few people wondered why I couldn't work during my time of healing. I tried to explain the pain was quite consistent, never letting up. There was seldom a moment when something, somewhere wasn't burning, stinging, throbbing, or itching. From morning to night, I had a regimen that included soaking 30 minutes at a time (four times a day) with the Domeboro (aluminum acetate) astringent solution. Then I would smear on the Silver Sulfadiazine Cream. Because it wasn't always absorbed in my skin, I would have to wait, undressed from the waist up, for the white film to dissolve before putting on RadiaPlex®Rx Gel. Afterward I would slip into a loose-fitting cotton T-shirt or one of Tom's old sport shirts. If I had excessive burning, I applied 99 percent aloe vera gel, which helped cool me off. Before going to bed for the night, I applied a thin layer of Aquaphor Gel, which would keep my skin from drawing while I slept. If I forgot, by morning I would be in a world of hurt just trying to lift my arm or bend to get out of bed. One night I awoke at five in the morning unable to go back to sleep. I started thinking about the burns and how surprised I was at myself, being able to treat my own wounds: wash the dead skin away, apply the bandages, and cope with the disfigurement. I've always been deeply afraid of burns.

Occasionally, I get e-mail surveys from friends that are designed to help you get to know each other better. Several of them have asked, "What are you most afraid of?" Usually people will respond with, death, spiders, snakes, losing my spouse, losing a child, and the like. Do you know what I would always answer? *Fire*. I think that fear goes back to when I was a young child living in Alaska. If you reside in an area where the temperatures go way below zero, you know fire can be a death sentence. I had a little friend named Skeeter who attended our church. One night in the dead of winter, with subzero temperatures outside, a fire broke out in Skeeter's log-cabin home. Have you ever seen what happens when you try to put out a fire with water in below-zero temperatures? Everyone made it out but Skeeter — he died in the fire. As a little girl, I couldn't think of anything more horrible. For years I tried to imagine what it must have been like for my friend, and my fear of fire grew.

Then, my cousin Paul was in a work-related accident where sulfur dioxide spewed over his body. He was in the burn hospital in St. Louis for months and months during the fall and winter months of 2001. Several times, his brother called me to go to my knees in prayer for Paul during his roller-coaster recovery. I grieved over his pain, his terrible wounds, and his suffering. His wife, Jan, was by his side daily. I admired that so much and wondered if I would have the stamina to do the same.

I was so scared the first time I went to visit Paul. How would I handle seeing him? Would I be able to show him my love and not rush out of his room? I had to register and scrub in, then I was clothed in hospital garb from head to toe. As I walked into his room, I saw he was mummified, wrapped head to toe in sterile cloths. He knew me (although later he couldn't remember I had been there) and motioned for me to come to his bedside. Ah, I was going to be okay. It appeared I was stronger than I had thought. I returned for subsequent visits, and Paul became one of my biggest supporters during my cancer journey, offering me words of encouragement and calling just to talk.

During that long night, a song, "God Leads Us Along," came to mind. My mother used to sing it as a solo when I was a young girl. I never thought much about the words, but as I lay in bed thinking about the burns, I started to sing:

In shady green pastures, so rich and so sweet,

God leads His dear children along;

Where the water's cool flow bathes the weary one's feet,

God leads His dear children along.

Chorus:

Some through the waters, some through the flood.

Some through the fire, but all thro' the blood;

Some through great sorrow, but God gives a song,

In the night season and all the day long.[5]

I rose from bed and went to the computer where I found a message from Fred Eicher, "This morning, I've been praying for your healing, and God told me to remind you your body is only a vessel. He reminded me of a vase of flowers. The vase by itself isn't complete, but once it is filled with beautiful flowers it takes on a whole new power and identity." In *2 Corinthians 4* we read, "But we have this treasure in jars of clay to show that this all-surpassing power is from God and not from us (*v.* 7)." And then, "Though outwardly we are wasting away, yet inwardly we are being renewed day by day. For our light and momentary troubles are achieving for us an eternal glory that far outweighs them all (*vv. 16–17*)."

In that day's mail I received a card from Juanice Chitwood titled "The Oak Tree:" It spoke of a mighty oak tree withstanding wind, its branches being stripped away and the bark torn to the point it was left bare. The oak remained standing while other trees around it fell. The wind addressed the oak and questioned how it could stay standing in spite of all being taken away. The oak replied it was because it had roots deep in the earth and until the wind had come, it wasn't sure how much it could endure. The oak found out it was stronger than it ever knew.

It was the same for me. I was stronger than I ever knew. I had lost my hair, my eyebrows, my eyelashes, my taste buds, my fingernails, and my toenails. I had lost a lot of weight. I no longer had feeling in my feet. I had experienced pain like I never thought possible. I had burns to my hands, thrush, low blood counts, and third-degree burns to my chest. After all was said and done, I hoped I wouldn't forget. I didn't *want* to forget one moment. I wanted to be able to look into the wide, fear-filled eyes of that precious one who had just received a similar diagnosis and say, "He is able." Because He is.

DAYS OF WONDER

I felt so good to be back at work full time and not have to schedule days off for recovery. I was very busy, and sales were up. I did tire easily, and by the time I would get home it was all I could do to put food on the table. I had a tendency to go about 60 miles an hour, and suddenly fatigue would hit me like a ton of bricks. "Where is a seat so I can sit down?"

A few days before my follow-up visit with the radiology oncologist, he had a nurse call to check on me. The conversation went something like this:

"Judy, the doctor has been very worried about you, and he asked me to give you a call to see how your burns are healing?"

"Well, Jessica," I said, "I'm really healing very well. I think you all are going to be very surprised at how well I'm doing."

"Really?"

"Yes, really."

"Okay. Well, we will see you on Tuesday."

I went in, and they ushered me straight back to the examination room where they handed me the little gown. I hadn't been decked out in my altogether more than a minute before the doctor tapped on the door.

When he came in he looked very somber and quietly ventured, "Well, Judy, how are things?"

I held the opening to the front of the gown tightly shut and looked him square in the eyes, "Doctor, you remember when I told you I had hundreds of people praying for me all over the world?"

He nodded.

"Well, I want you to prepare yourself because what I'm about to show you is an answer to those prayers. You aren't going to believe what you are about to see." With that, I opened the gown.

This man, this doctor who never smiled let alone laughed, stood before me in utter silence. Then he grinned, and I heard something I had never heard before: he laughed. It wasn't a little snicker either. It was a hearty, belly laugh.

I then realized the man had actually thought he had scarred me for life, and he had been beating himself up for letting the treatments go too far, damaging me far beyond what could ever heal. He immediately gave credit to the Silver Sulfadiazine Cream, saying it was an amazing salve and had remarkable powers to heal.

No sooner had I closed my gown than Leslie, the radiology nurse/technician, came into the room with her face scrunched in a tormented scowl, "Can I see? Is it very bad?"

I smiled, pulled the gown open again, and said, "Leslie, be the judge!" I wish I'd had a camera to capture her shocked surprise. Her eyes bugged out of her head, and her mouth flew open in a gasp. It was so much fun to witness their reactions. As I left the office, the doctor was still laughing. He said I didn't have to return for a visit for three months. As I slipped out the door, I noticed the jigsaw puzzle I had worked on the previous few weeks in the lobby had been replaced with a new one. Someone else would just have to put that one together.

Two weeks after my visit to the radiologist, I had my first appointment to see the oncologist since finishing the radiation treatments. He kindly asked me how I had fared with the blast sessions, and I explained my last treatments had been canceled due to the extensive burns. I asked him if he wanted to see the pictures, and he said he would. I was surprised at his reaction to the photos. I guess because he's a doctor, I thought he would be rather calloused at seeing my red, blistered burns. He wasn't. He moaned and groaned with each slide, which led me to think, he was just being sympathetic."

I told him the radiologist had attributed my healing to the ointments he had prescribed, but I thought it was due to answered prayer. The doctor said, "Hop up on the table, and let's take a look." I crawled on the examination table and pulled up my top so he could get a good look. He jumped back from me, and his face went ashen. He said, "I've never seen anything like this."

I asked, "Like what?"

He said, "Like your chest wall!"

"Is that good?"

"Well, yes! Judy, this is amazing. I've never seen anyone come back from third-degree radiation burns without major scaring. Your skin is like a baby's. Usually the skin becomes hard, almost like cardboard. Look! Yours is pink and soft like new skin. I've *never* seen healing like this. Never!"

I reiterated, "The radiologist thought it was due to the Silver Sulfadiazine Cream."

He sighed, "Look, Judy, it has to be prayer, because everyone I've seen has used the Silver Sulfadiazine Cream. No one had the results I'm looking at now."

My head was reeling with this news. We went on to discuss other issues, one being my port. I asked him when he thought I should have it removed. He paused and said the decision would be up to me. I mentioned when I had the port installed, they couldn't find any veins in my left hand and arm that hadn't blown out. I also recounted the surgical team having to use a vein in my neck. I asked, "Do veins regenerate?"

He said, "No. Usually they don't. Because of that I think you probably need to think about keeping the port for a couple more years. Of course, that means you have to come in every six weeks to have it flushed out, but the alternative could be a problem."

He added, "Judy, the type and stage of your cancer makes you at high risk for it to return. In fact, the odds it will return are a much greater percentage. You need the port."

As I left the office that day I pondered those words. I thought I had won the war, but I was beginning to realize it was just one battle in the war. I had other battles to face. I've known people who live defeated lives because they constantly expect something terrible to happen. Did I want to be like that? No, I decided, I did not. My main concern was that I not dwell on the "what if" but that I dwell on God's all consuming power to work miracles within me every day. I rose the next morning with a determination to take each day as it would come, knowing He had already won the battles, both now and to come, and had claimed victory on my behalf. I knew I couldn't take the journey by myself. I would have to depend on all those who had traveled the road with me to hold me accountable.

At our church, Tom and I sit on the first row of the back section, which makes it easy to stretch out our legs. That location had come in handy after knee and hip surgeries and provided a quick exit on Sundays, so I could rush out and grab a bite to eat before heading to work. That convenient spot also affords a good look at the back pews of the front section.

One Sunday, shortly after my visit with the oncologist, I noticed a couple sitting directly in front of us. For some reason, I couldn't take my eyes off them. Perhaps it was their body language, but I felt the Lord was trying to tell me something. Instead of dismissing the service following the sermon, the praise team led the congregation in a time of worship. The lights were lowered, and this palpable presence of the Lord descended as a powerful force. While we sang, I felt the urging of the Holy Spirit to speak to the woman in front of us to tell her the Lord wanted her to let Him fight her battles and her job was to rest. It takes nerve and a little sweat and tears to step out in faith for such an audacious task. However, I've learned over the years that if I'm not obedient to these callings, I'll be miserable. So, the minute I saw them start to leave, I rushed forward and whispered in her ear, "I have a word for you from the Lord."

She looked startled and nodded her head, "Okay."

I gave her the message. She stared at me and said, "Would you repeat that?" I did.

She looked at me sideways, "Do I know you?"

"No." I said.

"What is your name?"

"Judy."

"Do you know my battle?"

Suddenly, it came to me! I said, "Yes. You have breast cancer."

She said, "How did you know that?"

I said, "I know because I've been there, too."

"Breast cancer?"

I nodded, "Yes".

I returned to my seat, and when I looked up the couple continued to stand there. Shortly afterward we were dismissed. As I started to exit, I felt a hand on my shoulder. It was her. She leaned into me and said, "Thank you. Thank you so much. I'm resting and at peace already. Thank you for being obedient."

I really want to say *YES* to God no matter the call or the cost. I must never forget I'm here on this earth for one purpose only: to glorify my Maker in all things.

MOUNTAIN MAMA

As summer time was coming to a close, our friends Don and Donna Gunnoe offered to let us meet Trina half way between Kentucky and New Jersey at their cabin in West Virginia. Donna went with us, and we headed out from Shelbyville on a Thursday. We arrived in Lewisburg late afternoon where we stopped at the local Wal-Mart to stock up on food before heading up Rt. 219 to Renick and the mountain road to Auto. Ten more minutes climbing the mountain, and we were there. Trina couldn't leave New Jersey until after Maia had an appointment with her new pediatric cardiologist, so she was to join us later that night with the children.

I had told Trina she needed to call us from Lewisburg before heading toward Renick because when she got to the base of the mountain where we were to meet her at a closed gas station, she wouldn't have cell-phone service. She either forgot or didn't hear that part of my directions. We thought she would be calling around 10:15 PM, but we didn't get a call. We waited until almost 11:00, and Tom couldn't stand it anymore. He was worried she could be sitting in the dark at the bottom of the mountain waiting for us to escort her through the winding roads.

We drove down the mountain to find no one at the gas station. I told Tom we would just sit there and wait until midnight. We hadn't been there 10 minutes before her little Scion pulled in from the opposite direction. She rolled down her window when her car pulled even with ours, and I could tell she was tremendously relieved. She had expected us to be waiting when she arrived in Renick at 10:30. Then she realized her phone wouldn't work, so she had driven on through town and up the other side of the mountain, hoping she could get cell-phone reception. All was well, and we arrived safely back at the cabin before midnight. The grand-kids looked wonderful, and the next morning they were bright eyed and ready to start their day entertaining Grandma and Papa. We got to take Gideon swimming in the Greenbrier River at the base of the mountain. It turned out to be the best four days and a wonderful way to celebrate the end of my chemo and radiation.

We packed the car early Sunday morning and drove down the mountain to attend Mt. Hermon United Methodist Church, so we could thank the beautiful ladies of the congregation for the lovely prayer shawls they had knitted for both Maia and me. I wasn't sure what to expect since the last time I'd been in a Methodist church was more than 40 years earlier, and it had been quite liturgical — something I wasn't accustomed to. I thought to myself, *Surely a church that would send out such lovely shawls couldn't be that bad, right?* We felt right at home the minute we walked through the doors., Actually, before we walked through the doors a booth in the parking lot welcomed us to help ourselves to free locally grown garden vegetables.

Such lovely, warm, and friendly people I have seldom met. They were all so eager to make us feel comfortable. They used some of the old hymnals, singing many of my favorite songs from years ago. Then there were several testimonies. Donna stood and introduced us, telling the congregation about Maia and the good report she had recently received concerning her heart and health; then Donna mentioned the shawls and my triumph through the cancer treatments. They all clapped vigorously.

During the time for "meeting and greeting," those people took the instruction to heart! Every single person met and greeted every single other person there that morning. They hugged and back slapped for a good five or ten minutes. It was a king-size love fest, if I had ever seen one. The most precious moment came as the pastor's wife, who had personally made Maia's prayer shawl, was led to Trina's side. As she bent over Maia, tears filled her eyes and spilled onto her cheeks. She gently brushed her hands over our sweet granddaughter, whispering, "Oh, my, my, my! How precious you are." I had to turn away for fear I would burst out in a full-fledged ugly bawl.

The worship team led the church in some choruses, and people all around us were raising their hands in praise. The pastor called two women to the front of the church to stand in proxy for members who were seriously ill. As he anointed them and prayed, the entire congregation got up and formed a circle of faith. What a precious sight. No wonder those prayer shawls had been effective. They were backed by the prayers of some powerful warriors.

Earlier Donna had told us before the main sermon, the pastor would call the children up front to sit at his feet around the altar. Usually he brought a mystery item in a paper bag that he would use as an object lesson for the kids' sermon. Gideon had gotten very excited at the prospect he would get to go up front with the pastor, but, Trina looked worried. When I told Gideon he would be "helping" the pastor preach his sermon, Trina looked in horror and said, "Don't say that, Mom! There is no telling what he might do!" The appointed time came; the children scurried to the front and sat around the pastor. I could tell Trina was holding her breath. My goodness, I thought, what could a little five year old say to cause his mother to be petrified with dread?"

The pastor pulled something out of his bag, and I couldn't tell what it was because I was sitting too far back, but, the illustration and gist of the sermon had to do with making a mountain out of a mole hill. He discussed this for a few minutes, tying it in with Scripture, then he opened the floor to discussion. I could feel Trina tense up.

One little girl made a comment about returning to school, and another little boy said something about new clothes. We were almost home free! Then the unmistakable high-pitched voice of my grandson could be heard, "I think we need to inspire the Word of God more." he said. There was stunned silence as everyone took in what this precocious child had just uttered. There were a few small giggles, and the pastor stuttered, "Um . . . why, yes. That is correct. We do need to inspire the Word of God more." At that the children were dismissed to return to their pews. I could hear Trina breathe a sigh of relief.

The preacher then got serious as he preached an old-time message, even coming down off the platform to make his points clearer and more forceful. I thought I was back at an old-time camp meeting! We left immediately after the service to head for Kentucky, stopping for a meal at Tudor's Biscuit World before bidding Trina and the children farewell as we headed west, and they headed east.

HERE I STAND

✸

Fall approached, life had settled down, and my recovery was running smoothly. Thankfully, my hair began to come back, even though I struggled with the initial kink that sprouted once the first strands grew an inch or two. My toenails and fingernails were gradually reappearing, though lined with deep ridges representing every chemo treatment I'd received all those many months before.

My radiology oncologist was pleased with my healing and stamina, which seemed to be increasing day by day. Again, he very carefully went over what I needed to watch for, i.e., bone pain, nausea (liver cancer), headaches or dizziness (cancer in the brain). He also mentioned I needed to be watchful for any eraser-size bumps that might pop up on my chest wall. I hadn't heard of that as a possible recurrence, so I quizzed him for about five minutes. He looked at me and said, "Judy, have any of your doctors talked specifically to you about the odds of this returning within the next five years?"

I told him that he had mentioned early on something about percentages with and without radiation. He jumped up and pulled out a bar graph and pointed to a black bar for someone with my type of cancer, the stage and the size. There it was: 25 percent chance of recurrence. I looked at the doctor and said, "Well, I guess I have a 75 percent chance it won't return. Don't I?"

He smiled.

The next week I was called into my corporate office and told I no longer worked for the company. I must say my first reaction at losing my job was devastation. My second, was "I'm going to have weekends off!" I was blessed to work in the building industry for 17 years. I had the best of the real-estate world because when you work directly for a builder you get to stay in one spot, have a beautiful model to work from, incur no out-of-pocket expenses, and meet the nicest people in the world. Conversely, the hours were long, and I worked every weekend. Losing my job meant no more rushing out the door on Sunday mornings after church to get to work on time.

Knowing I no longer had my job thrust me into the lowest of lows; then I'd bounce up to the highest of highs. That particular day was Joel's birthday and normally my day off. I was supposed to have gone out to eat with my friend Donna. After leaving the office, I thought about going to Frankfort and right away clearing my personal items out of the office. Tom talked me out of that, insisting I needed to have the ear of a trusted friend to relax and eat, share, and receive encouragement. So we headed to The Cheddar Box for a bite. All the way to the restaurant, and as we sat eating, we discussed what the Lord might have in store for me.

I struggled to focus on our conversation. My mind kept wandering, but Donna understood and kept bringing me back to the subject at hand. We did discuss my writing a book, and we talked about my desire to speak to other women and groups about God's provision for me during the past year. I told her I really wanted to reach out to other women who might be going through major health issues, breast cancer specifically. I couldn't decide what comes first? The chicken or the egg? The book or the speaking? I was floundering.

As we ate and visited together, I glanced past Donna to a couple of ladies sitting in a booth across from us. I recognized Teresa Skeeters. Teresa and her husband had once been part of a Bible class we attended. When we had finished eating, I stepped over to greet her. She jumped up and very warmly gave me a hug, making over my gray pixie cut and asking how I was doing. I told her about losing my job and she asked, "What are you going to do?"

I told her I had thought about writing and I really felt I had a story to tell, whether written or oral. I mentioned my urge to share and encourage other women going through cancer. Teresa started to cry. She pointed to the woman sitting with her and introduced me to Carol. As Carol rose from the booth, I could tell she was wearing a wig. Could it be?

She looked at me and asked, "Are you Tom's wife?"

I told her I was, and she mentioned she knew him from her days playing the piano with The Master's Men. She said she was in the middle of chemo. Teresa then explained she wanted me to give Carol something, anything that would be of encouragement.

To this day I don't remember what I said to Carol. I do know it just flowed out of me with little effort. I walked over to Donna waiting at the cash register, "It has already begun." When I told her what had happened, she started to tear up.

We walked next door to a little gift shop, and as we browsed I saw a lady I thought looked familiar. She kept looking at me, and I gazed back. Finally I inquired, "Do I know you?"

She asked, "What is your name?" I told her and she gushed, "Oh, Judy! I didn't recognize you with your new hair color and style."

I laughed. She continued, "I'm Mrs. Walters. You sold us a patio home at Swan Pointe. We still live there, and I've wanted to see you for the longest time to tell you how much we've loved our home. You know, you were the one who helped us make the selections for our condo, and every time I walk through the front door I thank God I listened to you and didn't put green tile in the foyer."

Later, as I drove over to Frankfort I thought about the events of the previous couple of hours. It wasn't an accident Teresa and Carol were at the café the same time I was. It wasn't chance that put Mrs. Walters at the gift shop. It was divine providence because the Lord knew I needed to know He had a plan, and I had worth. I had meant something to those women. I wasn't a failure. My life had meaning.

I started to hyperventilate as I crossed over the city limits of Frankfort. I'm not sure why. Perhaps it was the thought of never making the daily trek again. Within minutes of walking into the model home, cars started pulling up to the curb and homeowners converged. They had become friends and wanted to give me a pat on the back and a hug to lift my spirits. Hearing the news of my dismissal, they were in as much shock as I was. I never felt so loved and appreciated. Some, who were traveling, called the office to wish me the best. All of them gave me a real ego boost.

WRINKLE-FREE
CHARLIE BROWN
☸

Almost a full year had lapsed since my last radiation treatment when I developed a terrible cough. There was congestion, too, that seemed to be centered in my upper lungs and throat. I didn't think much about it. At a visit with the oncologist, who listened to my chest, I was told it was just a mild cold that would pass in time. It didn't. In fact, it got so much worse I was having difficulty breathing. Tom kept asking me to see another doctor. I think he was tired of hearing my croupy cough echo off the walls of the house.

I was finishing up the last chapters of this manuscript when one day I came to the part where radiation treatments had been suspended due to my severe burns. The radiologist had gone over a list of what I needed to watch for in the coming months. At one point, he had said lung damage could occur several months out, and if I developed a cough, congestion, or difficulty breathing I should come to see him right away.

I called to make an appointment, and they asked me to come immediately. I was quickly diagnosed with radiation pneumonia and started on a full regiment of steroids: three pills, three times a day. Initially, I didn't have side effects other than the immediate clearing of the cough and congestion. What a blessing! I was told even though my symptoms had disappeared, it was important to continue the regimen because the cough could return, and I might risk permanent lung damage.

All went well until the end of the second week when I began having difficulty sleeping — wrong choice of words. Actually, I didn't sleep. Through four nights I stared at the ceiling. Several people offered me "natural" sleeping aides, but nothing helped until I relented and took one of the sleeping pills Tom kept on hand and used once or twice a week. I immediately called the radiology oncologist to see if I could get a prescription for the same drug, and he referred me to my internist who ordered the medication for me.

After three weeks I was allowed to reduce the dosage of the steroids to two tablets twice a day. About that time, I experienced another side effect: the swelling of my face and my arms. I didn't go mad eating everything in sight (one of the most common side effects) because the Prednisone caused me to have mild nausea. The positive side effect was having unbelievable energy, pep, and tremendous "get up and go." Additionally, all my fibromyalgia pain disappeared. For the first time in years, I was pain free except for a nagging backache and some foot discomfort. I was pain free! I never realized how close to being an invalid I'd been. I could actually roll over in bed without having every muscle in my body scream in agony.

My house had never been so clean. We have a huge storage closet that became the drop-off for box after box of "kids' stuff" when we moved to our house eight years prior. We had added boxes from my parent's home when my mother's place sold and even more when she died. These boxes had been shuffled around and made to look orderly but never opened and their contents sorted. Finally, they were all sorted, and the storage room cleaned from top to bottom. Goodwill benefited from most of the clothing, and everything was neatly stacked in plastic containers, labeled, and easily accessible. The storage room was a masterpiece of glorious proportion and large enough we could potentially set up a good-size bowling alley for the grandchildren. I cleaned out and rearranged another closet, and my pantry resembled what I imagined Martha Stewart might consider a proper example of perfection. I just couldn't stop cleaning, arranging, adjusting, or decorating. I'd sit down only to jump up again to tackle another household chore.

Then, the insomnia returned. I went back to the doctor, and he reduced the steroid dosage; he put me on one pill twice a day but warned if the cough returned, he would have to increase the dosage again. The swelling in my face got worse. People were starting to notice, so on my own, I decided I would chance taking only one pill in the morning. It seemed to work. The swelling started going down, but the cough came back. The congestion returned. I had to go back to the twice-a-day schedule, consequently, the swelling returned in full force.

I knew from my many months on chemo one of my biggest faults was vanity. I did everything I could to disguise the ravages of chemotherapy on my outer appearance, and I succeeded in fooling a lot of the people most of the time. But hiding the swelling in my face? I couldn't disguise that even with contouring makeup. It wasn't going to happen.

While picking up a prescription, I asked to speak with the head pharmacist. "I think I know the answer to this question," I mused, "but, I need to know if there is anything on the market that might counteract the side effects I'm experiencing from steroids."

She looked at me and, shaking her head from side to side, said, "No. There is nothing."

I asked if she knew how long after discontinuing the steroid treatment it would take for the swelling to abate. She replied, "I've known some who never have it disappear. For some, it takes several months."

Then a guy standing next to her said, "I had a friend whose face blew up twice his normal size, and his neck area below his chin became enormous. After he stopped the steroids, the swelling in his face gradually went down but not his neck, and now it hangs down onto his chest."

If looks could have killed, he would be dead right now. I was mortified. I turned to walk away and I looked at Tom in stunned agitation, "Did you hear that?"

He tried to be encouraging, "Judy, you have an angular face anyway, so the roundness isn't that bad. It just makes you look really healthy." Tom is still alive, but he rates right below the guy behind the counter on my endangered list.

This whole steroid experience was an unexpected twist in the cancer saga. It was just another way the cancer haunted me. I didn't want to become a hermit, cooped up in my house, afraid of what people would say if I ventured out. The bravery I championed throughout my year of treatments seemed to have vanished. The only good thing I could see coming from this new challenge was that with each puffy cheek, my wrinkles were erased. Instead of an aging 64 year old, I looked like a wrinkle-free Charlie Brown.

At about that point in the steroid regimen, I began to notice my hair was getting thinner and thinner. I couldn't recall anyone connecting hair loss with steroid use. I got on the computer and looked up the side effects. Sure enough, there it was . . . *baldness*. I thought, Oh, dear, here we go again. Of course, my dear husband was more practical about the problem, saying I would have a good opportunity to get more mileage out of the three wigs I had purchased the year before.

While I was looking up *steroids,* I noticed a little side bar that talked about reducing the dosage too quickly. I clicked on it and found out my little experiment the previous week (cutting back on my own, which resulted in the cough and congestion returning) was a big, big NO, NO! My doctor had failed to mention the primary consequence of reducing steroid use too rapidly can cause Addison's Disease. Looking up *Addison's* I immediately went into panic mode.

Addison's is an illness that attacks the adrenal system, shutting down the kidneys and other organs that might mean the "patient" would need kidney dialysis and/or die. When the nurse from the radiologist's office called to see how I was doing and to remind me of my next appointment, I confessed what I had done and the results. Furthermore, I acknowledged I had gone back to the full dosage: one pill, twice a day, which seemed to take care of the problem. She made it very clear I would have to "fess up" to the doctor as well when I visited the office. I certainly dreaded having to confess to him. You would think over the years I'd become quite accomplished at revealing my sins, but I was not looking forward to facing the doctor with my misdeed.

It turned out not to be too bad. My face was quite swollen, and the doctor was very empathetic. We came up with a plan to reduce the dosage by half a pill for the time being, but if the cough returned, rather than again increasing the dosage, I would be given a codeine cough suppressant (with pretty powerful side effects in and of itself). I started on the half-pill reduction, and the cough didn't return. Then I reduced another half pill until I was put on just a half pill a day. The cough never returned. Thankfully, the plan worked. My round face gradually deflated but it took a full year before I could look in the mirror and see my former self. My neck remains where it was originally.

LIVING FORWARD, UNDERSTANDING BACKWARD

❀

Throughout my year of trusting, my friends sent me cards, e-mails, and letters that encouraged and uplifted me even through the roughest moments. One of the best was from Fred Eicher. The day I wrote about wanting a "do over" he e-mailed me his devotional for the day, which certainly hit the nail on the head.

It was a story about a man, who in his 20s participated in a wilderness training course in a mountainous desert region. For their last exercise they were blindfolded, put in the back of a pickup truck, then moved to a remote area, and left stranded. They were given three days to meet back at the main camp. They didn't know where they were and had to rely solely on their compasses. Needless to say, the four of them were very frightened. It had snowed that morning and trudging through the terrain was hazardous. They walked through valleys, canyons, hills and forests. Taking three days to go 60 miles, many times they didn't think they could go any farther. They were exhausted and frostbitten by the time they made it to the base camp. At the end of their adventure they stood on top of a ridge and looked behind themselves to see the beautiful land they had traveled. Then the pain of what they had just endured waned. For the first time they felt a sense of accomplishment.

Life is very much like this training exercise. It is often lived forward, (as we struggle through the thickets and the obstacles, never sure of where we are,) but understood backward (as we view the landscape with a new appreciation for its particular beauty and lasting effects). We have to be down the road a bit before we can appreciate the journey. I'm not at the point where I can look back and "breathe a sigh of relief," but I can say one day I will.

These days Maia is a lively toddler with little residual effects from the heart problems which plagued her at birth. The doctors still keep a close eye on her and haven't ruled out additional treatments or procedures but for the time being she thrives. She has limited use of her left hand and walks with a slanted gait; possibly the result of a stroke sometime during the first year of her life.

Kaya, likewise, shows all the typical signs of a well adjusted child; living and learning in the style of a healthy rambunctious youngster.

Just as I had desired at the beginning, the Lord graciously sent people to me who needed the voice of assurance from one who had been there. I have been honored to sit with those undergoing their own chemotherapy treatments; to provide answers to their questions, and give them a sense of hope in the midst of the storm that appears to be threatening their boat.

I accompanied a dear friend recently as she had her first chemotherapy for lung cancer. She was reclining in "my chair," the one I occupied the first day of my treatments. This time, I was looking at the chair instead of sitting in it. This time I was looking forward and understanding backward.

When I sold patio homes I got in the habit of always checking the obituary column in the daily papers to see if someone I had assisted in purchasing, or someone I had met through my real-estate dealings, had died. These days I've added to the list and watch for names and pictures of those I've met during the long days in the treatment center. Occasionally I'll see a familiar face and my heart sinks. The lady I met my first day of chemotherapy was pictured recently but Lisa's has not been there. I hear she is doing quite well and still gets frequent check-ups and blood work at the lab.

I would never assume my story is exceptional. It was a journey fraught with numerous battles but He never let go and I stand victorious. Many of my friends, before and after, struggled through cancer and had different outcomes. It is a fickle disease which defies explanation but walking through the valley of the shadows can offer an insight of God's mercies more glorious than any words can speak.

I didn't want to get into the boat the Lord had waiting. I could see the storm clouds gathering on the horizon and knew it was going to be a bumpy ride. It could very well have been a journey I would not survive. But I didn't have a choice because He MADE ME get in the boat. I had to launch out into the deep and trust in my maker to bring me through or carry me to glory.

God is good all the time. He reigns and showers us with blessings beyond what we ask or deserve. I don't know how anyone going through a life-threatening illness can face each day without the saving grace of Jesus Christ. He is more precious to me today than when I started my journey and He

grows sweeter with each passing moment. I know in whom I

trust for He will never let go – no, He never let go. In whom

do you put your trust?

ENDNOTES

1. May Christ Be Seen In Me, by Lois Dehoff, copyright 1941, by Percy Crawford

2. The Miracle Arrival – poem by Lil Walters, 10-29-08, used by permission.

3. Turn Your Eyes Upon Jesus,by Helen H. Lemmel, 1922, Public Domain

4. Every Hour and Every Day, by Marshall Pack, Gospeltone Music Publishing 1965

5. God Leads Us Along, by George A. Young, 1903, Public Domain

Author web site: www.getintheboat.com